SPELL BY WRITING

Wendy Bean
Chrystine Bouffler

Primary English Teaching Association
NSW, Australia

Heinemann
Portsmouth, New Hampshire

Heinemann Educational Books, Inc.
361 Hanover Street   Portsmouth, NH 03801
Offices and agents throughout the world

Copyright © Primary English Teaching Association, 1987
PO Box 167   Rozelle NSW 2039   Australia

First U.S. printing 1991

Library of Congress Cataloging-in-Publication Data
Bean, Wendy
    Spell by writing / Wendy Bean, Chrystine Bouffler.
       p. cm.
    Reprint. Originally published: 1987.
    Includes bibliographical references (p.   ).
    ISBN 0-435-08577-8
    1. English language--Orthography and spelling--Study and teaching
(Primary) 2. English language--Composition and exercises--Study and
teaching (Primary) 3. Interdisciplinary approach in education.
I. Bouffler, Chrystine. II. Primary Teaching Association
(Australia) III. Title
LB1526.B48   1991
372.6'32--dc20

                                        90-27028
                                            CIP

Cover painting: Isto Jakola
Design consultant: Mark Jackson
Editor: J.V. Steele
Typeset in 10/12 Sabon by Dovatype
53-37 Cambridge Street, Collingwood 3066

Printed in the United States of America
91 92 93 94 95 9 8 7 6 5 4 3 2 1

Contents

Acknowledgements

Books such as this are not possible without the help of a great many people. We would particularly like to acknowledge the work of Carolyn Burke, which has informed so much of our classroom practice. To the students and staff of Kooringal Public School, Wagga Wagga, our debt is immeasurable. The many other teachers and children who have shared experiences with us also deserve our thanks. They are too numerous to mention individually. To all language learners, to Megan who gave us hope and Ben who taught us faith, this book is dedicated.

Introduction

HOW THIS BOOK CAME INTO BEING

In recent years the teaching of writing has undergone something of a revolution, prompted by the work of Donald Graves, with the intention of focusing on process, not product. This revolution has come to be called 'process writing'—an unfortunate name, since it neither indicates the true nature of the revolution nor allays fears that it is just another teaching fad. Revolutions invariably give rise to uncertainty, and in such a climate 'process writing' has taken on all the elements of a teaching method. When this happens certain classroom practices become prescribed. In the minds of many classroom teachers a 'process-writing' classroom is one where children must be allowed to choose their own topics for writing, where pieces are drafted and redrafted, where teachers conference with children rather than correct work, and where children's writing is published.

I was not entirely immune to these orthodoxies, as Graves has called them, and like many teachers who embraced 'process-writing' I was faced by a series of problems for which solutions were not readily found. They included the following.

How does a teacher conference 30 children?

I had so many enthusiastic writers that I felt I was losing control of my preferred orderly classroom. Children were lining up for conferences and I was concerned that some children would miss out. At first I thought this was a fault of the program, but I came to realise that it was purely an organisational issue, though not an easy one to deal with. Classroom management strategies which had worked before had to be critically evaluated. Very clear objectives needed to be set, at times challenging past practices that had been both comfortable and successful.

What do you do in a conference?

As strategies were developed to organise conferences for the children, what actually occurred in this precious time became an issue. Dealing with the content and the surface features of the writing, particularly spelling, concerned me. So, too, did record keeping: how could I store enough information to justify what was happening if I was challenged at any time? It seemed possible that some children might go unnoticed for a while, and although they all were busy writing, I could not be certain of every child's progress and needs. However, over a period of time various management strategies were implemented, and they will be described later in the book.

How do you avoid becoming a verbal red pen?

My first reaction was to do orally what may in the past have been done with a red pen. I seemed to want to deal first with the surface features of the writing. Quite often with beginning writers the errors were numerous, and how could a teacher justify all the 'mistakes' that remained if only some were dealt with? Wouldn't the children continue to make these errors if they were left? There seemed to exist a belief that if children saw an incorrect spelling they would learn it. At the same time I believed it would be better to deal with just a few teaching points in each piece of writing, and was still concerned with how that might appear to an outsider.

Is it wrong to set topics?

It seemed that there were occasions when it would be appropriate to set a topic, but when were these occasions, and how often should I do it? What about this control the children were supposed to have over their own writing, and how did they learn to have it? I wondered when to intervene with the child showing no progress. What of the child writing only story? Context for writing soon became an important factor in my thinking about these issues.

How many drafts should children do?

Much was being written about Writing and how it was being treated in classrooms. I heard of two-draft classrooms and four-draft classrooms, which seemed to be based on simplistic interpretations of what was being written. None the less I was confused about the variety of all the things happening under the name of 'process writing'. Each child's control of the process was very different: some needed to redraft, some did not. The physical chore of redrafting made others less enthusiastic to continue. I needed a better understanding of the process to make decisions about individual children.

Should everything be published?

The issue of publication was a big one. While it was the process that was important, there seemed to be a lot of emphasis on publishing. As I talked to teachers, it became apparent that the making of little books for the children was becoming some sort of measure of what was happening in the classroom. The children in my room certainly enjoyed this end result of their efforts for a while, but it was not as important as it seemed. The need for variety in their writing was already apparent. They needed guidelines too, but again their varying abilities asked for individual treatment.

What about the children whose work is not good enough to publish ?

Lots of things were being written by the children, but many of their efforts were not suitable for publication. Was I still supposed to make such decisions ? What of the children still unable to produce writing suitable for an audience ? If they weren't publishing, what should happen to their growing pile of material ? How could I help maintain their interest ?

Should the teacher exert any editorial control before something is published ?

Young children do not have editorial skills and so these need to be taught and practised. But as these skills developed, my children could still only edit to the limit of their ability. What then ? Did it become my responsibility, or was I interfering with the process ? At this stage I came to realise that there are differences between editing and proofreading. These differences may be small but they are important for the emerging writer. The children needed expertise in both. Strategies were required to help them become effective proofreaders and hence better spellers. I began to see children developing a spelling consciousness which seemed to be basic to being a good speller.

What about Spelling ? How do you teach it ?

This became the biggest issue of all. Spelling was an isolated subject in my classroom and was being treated quite separately from reading and writing. The children were good spellers on the whole—or so I could assume from the results of spelling tests—but there was little carry-over to their writing. My dissatisfaction grew, and in my attempts to solve this problem I invited Dr Bouffler to work in my classroom.

It was in this climate that we began some action research. We started with a group of thirty Kindergarten, Year 1 and Year 2 children in a vertical group. Dr Bouffler worked regularly with me and the children for the school year. Since then we have worked together in a variety of situations, and while our work began with young children, it now has an Infants-Primary perspective. Our observations have taught us a great deal about language learning, much of which we would now like to share with other educators.

Although this book was born of the attempt to solve the problem of spelling, in the process many other dilemmas were solved—dilemmas represented by the questions being asked by many teachers besides myself. The answers were sought both in and out of the classroom, and the process became like the unravelling and reknitting of a garment. One question invariably led to another, so that the concern for spelling in relation to writing became a concern for all facets of language. The children constantly demonstrated the interrelationship between reading and writing. It was obvious that much of their knowledge about spelling came from their reading. They would often turn to books they had read to solve their spelling problems, and certainly what and how they wrote reflected what they had read. What emerged was, in fact, a total language program. 'Process writing' became not just a methodology but the process of writing—and a way of viewing, not just writing, but *all language*.

Wendy Bean

Chapter One

LANGUAGE, WRITING AND SPELLING

'How do we assist children to learn?' That is the fundamental question teachers face. We put the emphasis on learning because a teacher can only provide the conditions for learning. Learners in any situation are ultimately responsible for their own learning.

There are many factors which help teachers to answer the question when assisting learners of language. The two most important are:

- what we understand about language, and
- what we understand about learners, especially those in the classrooms in which we work.

The following diagram suggests how these factors are related.

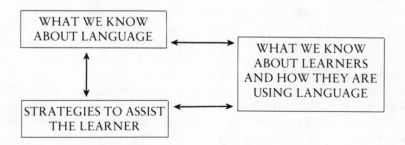

All teachers know something about the things they are teaching and the way children learn. That 'something' may be a lot or a little, well articulated or intuitive. It may also be sound or based on false assumptions. But whatever it is, it determines in no small measure what goes on in the classroom. It enables teachers to make judgements about children's performances and develop teaching programs. It is reflected in the classroom practices chosen and the day-to-day running of the classroom.

Answering the question of how to assist language learners depends upon having sound assumptions about language and learning. We started with what we believed were sound and clear understandings, but found as we worked with children that some of them needed constant revision and clarification. This was particularly the case with our beliefs about writing and spelling. We firmly believed that spelling was part of the writing process, and in attempting to grapple with what this meant in classroom practice, we came to realise that there were gaps in our understanding of writing. Current thinking, while it provided many valuable insights, did not provide us with a model that worked for us, and so we needed to develop our own.

In the course of our work together two things became very clear to us. The first was that 'teaching' spelling is as much about 'teaching' reading and writing as it is about spelling *per se*. The second was what all teachers know but are reluctant to accept: that there is no instant recipe for teaching anything. The best we can do is to share with you the beliefs we have about language in its various manifestations and about how it is learned, and then share some of the teaching strategies we have used, which we believe are significant in learning to write and spell.

Although the teaching strategies may well be the most interesting part of the book to many teachers, it is important that those who find the strategies useful understand the thinking about language, especially reading and writing, that underpins them. It is this understanding, not the strategies themselves, that gives teachers control in their classrooms. No two classrooms are the same, and so no teaching strategy is necessarily appropriate for each class or all children in a class. Some of our best teaching strategies may go unused and we may be forced to develop others. It is our understanding of language and language development, together with what we know of the children in our classes, that helps us to develop teaching strategies and to decide which are appropriate. It is this understanding that we fall back on when faced with such questions as, 'Why isn't this working?', 'Where do I go next?', 'What materials will I buy?'. Therefore we consider it important to begin with our understandings of language and learning.

Language

Language is used by people for specific purposes in a wide variety of contexts. As Halliday (1975) puts it, it is *functional*, *social* and *contextual*. Learning a language means learning to use a language. In fact, language only exists in use. The people with whom we use it, the purposes for which we use it and the contexts in which we use it—all determine what kind of language we use and the way it is understood.

The basic purpose of language is to sign meaning. Language is the principal vehicle for making sense of our world and conveying meaning to others. Accordingly it would seem self-evident that the only way children can effectively learn language is by being exposed to it in meaningful situations, and by having opportunities to experiment with it and use it. The need to make sense is what activates and 'drives' language learning.

The language that children learn is determined by their life circumstances. Because children come from a particular culture, the language they learn and speak will be the language peculiar to that culture. To the extent that they come from, or move between particular sub-groups within the culture, their language will reflect the language of those sub-groups. Finally, because each is an individual, there will be that about their language which is peculiar to the individual.

The school is one such sub-group, and in order for children to succeed at school they must become successful users of school language. This in turn means that school language situations must be meaningful and encourage children to experiment with and use language purposefully.

It is appropriate at this point to make one other comment about learners which, we believe, is true of all learning situations, and not just language learning. It explains much about our approach to language in the classroom. It concerns the learners' control of their own learning. Teachers can guide learners but the learner must do the learning. However, giving control to the learner does not mean giving licence to children to do what they will with the language. In order to give control to learners we may have to place limitations on what they can do. For example, it is no good giving children freedom to write stories about whatever they wish if they have no idea of what constitutes a story. We have to help them to at least a rudimentary understanding of story before they can have any control over writing stories. To do this may require teaching strategies which appear to limit freedom. For instance, it may be appropriate to restrict the choice of topic, or the type of text children write, until such time as they have the knowledge to exercise a reasonable measure of control. If you give learners the beginning of a story and ask them to complete it, you are in a sense restricting their freedom to choose their own topics and the type of text they write. Such restriction may be desirable in terms of giving the learner control in a story-writing situation. We would not ask a learner who cannot yet drive to take us from A to B in peak-hour traffic. The usual procedure is to restrict learner drivers to an area that minimises the likelihood of damage until they have some control over the car.

Giving the learner control does not, therefore, mean lack of teacher control, as has been claimed by opponents of 'process writing'. It is the teacher who guides the learning by creating situations in which learning can take place. It is the teacher who must decide whether or not a learner is in control and, if not, create circumstances in which control can be exercised. Unfortunately many teachers, ourselves included, have sometimes lacked the knowledge to enable us to exercise this kind of control in the classroom. In some cases young writers have been out of control because we did not understand how to give them control. The criticism has been justified. The answer, however, lies not in returning to old methodologies, but in developing our understanding of how we can assist learners to control their own learning.

Writing

What you believe about language in general must also be true for the manifestations of language such as writing, and writing of course includes spelling. The problem lies in making the connections. Briefly, these connections are summarised in the following table.

Language is . . .	**Writing** is **language**. It is . . .	**Spelling** is **language**. It is . . .
Functional We use language to organise our world, to communicate, to *mean*. Because we need to do these things in order to function, we learn language.	**Functional** We write in order to create *meaning* over time, to explore ideas, to remember something, to communicate.	**Functional** It is a system for recording *meaning*. Spelling serves no purpose except as part of the writing process.
Social Language is used by people and between people. Every speaker assumes a listener, every reader a writer, and so on.	**Social** Writers assume readers. Sometimes we are our own readers, e.g. when we write shopping lists for ourselves.	**Social** Spelling enables readers to reconstruct meaning. Standard spelling assists the reader. Communities determine what is standard.
Contextual We use language in a variety of contexts. These shape the language we use and the meaning we construct. Language exists only in use.	**Contextual** Situations demand that we write. Why we write, what we write, to whom we write and the kind of text we write are determined by the context in which we write.	**Contextual** Contexts in which we write shape the way we spell. In some contexts standard spelling is important, in others it is less so. We use standard spelling if we have the need to use it.

In order to appreciate how writing is functional, social and contextual, it is necessary to consider writing in more depth.

There is little doubt that our understanding of the writing process is less well developed than our understanding of other language processes. It is simply much harder to study, and people in general write less often than they talk, listen or read. Theorists such as Flower & Hayes (1980) and Nancy Shanklin (1982) provide valuable insights, but these are not easily translated into working models for teachers.

The person who has most influenced current thinking about writing in this country is Donald Graves. Although Graves is mainly concerned with the learning and teaching of writing, his work has been underpinned by the insights of Donald Murray. Murray (1982) divides writing into a number of recursive stages —*rehearsing*, *drafting* and *revising*. He points out that writers do not necessarily 'get it right' the first time. Writing involves discovering one's meaning and drafting and redrafting to make it clear. There is no doubt that this view has done much to assist classroom practice, but as we worked with the children in our classroom we discovered its limitations.

It seemed to us that Murray's view of writing better suited certain kinds of text, particularly stories. But how did it accommodate such things as personal letters or shopping lists, those one-off texts that we sometimes produce? Perhaps it might be argued that the rehearsing, drafting and revising go on in our heads before the text appears on the page. However, the notion of recursive stages did not seem to fit with what we ourselves did as writers or what children often did. It seemed that these 'stages' often went on simultaneously. At first we thought that this impression stemmed from bad practice, but the children taught us otherwise. Finally, as we observed children and reflected on our own writing process, we became convinced that any view of writing must take into account the effect of the writing context on the shape of the process. For this reason we developed our own view of the process.

Writing is, first of all, a response to a social situation which contains the need to write. This is simply another way of saying that writing is functional, social and contextual. We write because we have a need to convey meaning over time and writing is the appropriate way of doing it. This may seem to be very much a statement of the obvious, but we found that in a classroom it is very easy to lose sight of this essential fact. Writing can easily become writing for writing's sake, or, worse still, writing only for some form of teacher assessment.

As we see it, writing may have a number of aspects—*focusing, composing, editing* and *proofreading*. These may be equated with Murray's rehearsing, drafting and revising. The term *focusing* is used, however, to capture Frank Smith's (1982) notion of global and specific focus, and because, for us, rehearsing carries the idea of something you do before the real thing. We start with a global focus—an idea that we will write about something. We then go through various narrowings of that focus to the paragraph, the sentence, the word. Through this narrowing of focus our original global focus becomes refined, even changed. *Composing* and *editing* refer to the business of developing and refining meaning. *Proofreading* involves making sure the surface features of the writing are standard. It may be somewhat artificial to separate editing and proofreading, but the distinction has proved particularly useful in dealing with issues of standard spelling.

These activities may occur simultaneously when we write—indeed they frequently do. How often do we find ourselves editing the moment something appears on the page, or correcting spelling as soon as it is written? At any one particular point in the process, however, one or other of these activities will be emphasised. A metaphor may help to explain this. Imagine a dance floor filled with dancers. While the music plays the dancers keep moving. There is a spotlight which plays across the dance floor and every so often comes to rest on a group of dancers. The action under the spotlight becomes highlighted for a time but the rest of the dancers continue, unless the action under the spotlight becomes all absorbing. So we may be constantly focusing, composing, editing and proofreading during the process of writing, but at any one time one of these aspects of the process will be under the spotlight.

What determines the point of attention—where the spotlight falls, so to speak? The answer is simply the *context*, i.e. the sum total of the circumstances in which the writing takes place. It is the context that determines if we write and what we write. It includes such things as the subject and content of the message being written, the relationship between the writer and the audience, and the form of the message. We have found it useful to think of the context in terms of topic, audience, purpose and type of text, although we recognise that to do so is, from a linguistic viewpoint, an over-simplification. Nevertheless it provides a manageable starting point.

Topic, audience, purpose and type of text are interdependent. Decisions a writer makes about one affect the others. If the writing is to serve as a memory aid in the supermarket, then the writer is hardly likely to produce a poem called 'Reflections on Weeds in a Garden'! Decisions made by the writer concerning topic, audience, purpose and type of text also determine the shape of the writing process.

When we are writing a shopping list, it is doubtful that we do much editing or proofreading. It is of little consequence in this context whether or not we know the standard spelling of 'spaghetti' (though the situation may be different if someone else is to do the shopping). On the other hand an article for a teachers' journal may require a lot of composing, editing and proofreading before the writer submits it. Because context shapes the writing process, views of writing that do not consider it are inadequate and a poor base for classroom practice. Our own experience with young writers also suggests that children can begin to make decisions about context at an early age, which is not surprising after all, since all writing takes place in context. It is important, therefore, that teachers encourage this decision making and develop it as children progress through school.

The view of writing expressed here can be summed up in the following diagram:

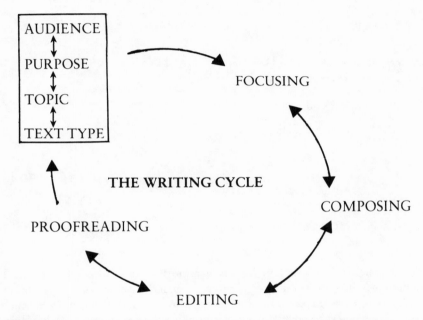

But while diagrams are useful, they have their limitations. They are by nature linear, and there is a danger that as a result the writing process will be viewed linearly. Writing has progression but it is not a linear process. How the various aspects of the process relate together is determined by the context, which varies from one piece of writing to another, and this should always be borne in mind when interpreting the diagram.

Spelling

Where does spelling fit within our view of language and the model of writing we have presented? To answer this question, it's necessary to explore some understandings about spelling. The table on p.7 suggests that since spelling is an aspect of language, it is also functional, social and contextual. Such an assertion challenges some deeply held traditions.

Because spelling is part of the written language system, it serves the needs of both writers and readers. It enables the writer to record meaning and the reader to reconstruct that meaning. To do this spelling must be systematic. But while standard spelling is systematic, spelling does not necessarily have to be standard to be systematic or to be read. Standards change over time and across language groups, although many people are reluctant to accept that they do. The following text demonstrates some interesting facts about reading and spelling. Five-year-old Jason was very insistent that his class should sing 'Puff the Magic Dragon' and wanted his teacher, Elaine Lloyd, to write up the words. Elaine did not get it done soon enough for Jason and so he produced his own attempt.

Pof   the   mateck   traon   Lefd   Bie
the   se   and   in   frolet   in   te
orm   mese   in   a   land   cod
on   a   led   letol   tace
    PaePoh   Love   tat   rasa
    Paf   and   Bort   tlem   faz
    and   Sele   Wos   and   Los   of
    fanse   saf   ho   Paf   the
    mateck   tracn   Lefd   Bie   the   se   and
    frolet   en   te   orm   mest   in a
    land   coda   on   a   led

What we bring to the reading process is as important as what is on the page. Thus most people who know the song can read Jason's version with a minimum of difficulty, despite the fact that most of it is non-standard. But a reader who does not know the song will scarcely make it out from this version. The point is that there are many factors which affect the reading of a text. Spelling is but one. Non-standard spelling does not necessarily affect our ability to read something.

It is because spelling is very much a social activity that we have standard spelling. Standard spelling makes text more predictable for readers. We know what to expect and are saved the necessity of discovering the writer's system, as we need to do in Jason's case. But making it easier for the reader may make it harder for the writer, particularly for young learners. If Jason's teacher had insisted on standard spelling, he would never have produced this piece of writing, and we would probably never have discovered just what he knows about spelling. Although most of his spelling is non-standard, he already has an excellent control over spelling conventions: almost all the letter clusters he uses are to be found in English.

We must also face the fact that there are very strong social pressures for standard spelling. Standard spelling and punctuation are very often the measures by which levels of literacy and writing ability are judged. Regardless of one's personal reactions, no teacher can afford to ignore this. However, recognition must be tempered by the realisation that, like all language, spelling is context specific.

There is a tendency to believe that spelling is automatic: once you know how to spell a word (and that means knowing the standard form) you will spell it that way each time you use it. But this is not necessarily true. The circumstances of our writing may well affect the way we spell. Consider what happens to spelling when you are taking notes. How often do children produce standard spelling in a list but not when they write the same word in a text? Changing our stance from that of a writer to that of a reader can alter our perception of spelling. How often have you come back to a text you have written and, in the process of re-reading it, discovered non-standard spelling?

What we believe about spelling can be related to our model of writing. If we look at the model, we can see that there are two points at which spelling is important in the writing process. The first is that point where we put meaning on the paper—when we start to compose. Here spelling should assist, not hinder the writer's attempt to make meaning clear. The second point occurs when we become readers of our own writing and look at its surface features to ensure, where it is demanded, that they are standard. This part of the process is called proofreading and it is here that issues of standard spelling are highlighted. In the past we have taken the ability to proofread for granted. Somehow, if you could read, you could proofread. But there are subtle differences between reading and proofreading which children need to learn, and we have devoted a chapter to discussing these differences and how to help children become proofreaders.

Most efficient writers have sufficient control over standard spelling to make it serve their needs both as readers and writers. For most English speakers there is no problem in producing an English spelling, i.e. one that obeys the rules of English orthography, but for some there may well be a problem in knowing which, among the possible spellings of a word, is standard. The problem of teaching spelling, as we see it, is largely one of helping children to know what is standard. Initially they may need help in representing words with letter strings that are acceptable in English. Once they can do this, they need help to become standard spellers, and this requires them to become both effective readers and proofreaders.

Chapter Two

LANGUAGE AND SPELLING DEVELOPMENT

While it is true to say that our beliefs about language, writing and spelling were extended and refined by our classroom experiences, our approach to the problem of spelling was governed, in general, by the principles outlined in the first chapter. We were acutely aware that traditional methods of teaching spelling were at odds with our beliefs about language. If language exists only in use, then it must be learned in use. It is not and never can be learned by memorisation. What we know of the limitations of short-term and long-term memory would support this. At best, memorisation may account for perhaps several hundred spelling words. It certainly cannot account for the thousands of words in the repertoire of the average literate person.

Apart from our theoretical objection to memorising spelling lists, we found that the children considered the spelling lists did not fit with their writing. One second grader, when asked why words that were standard in her spelling list were not standard in her writing, said simply, 'That's spelling. This is writing.' Talking with children about their perceptions of writing and spelling suggested that many of them made similar distinctions.

As a matter of policy the Quota spelling scheme was used throughout the lower grades of the school. This program adopts what is essentially a list approach. Words are grouped loosely on a phonic basis. Children are pre-tested and assigned a particular quota, passing on to the next when they have satisfactorily learned the previous one. Although the idea is that children work at their own pace, there is always the danger that quotas become competitive because of peer or parental pressure.

Our first task was to seek support from senior staff and parents for abandoning the Quota system. This support was crucial. Because many parents expect that children will be given lists of words to learn, they feel the school is failing in its job if such lists are not brought home. They also need to be reassured that children will develop standard spelling without them. After all, they believe they learned through lists. Without the support of parents it is very difficult to implement the writing/reading program described in this book.

Classroom activity cannot cease while teachers are finding solutions to their teaching problems, and so our first step was to get the children writing and simply observe what they did when they were confronted by spelling problems. Three things then become apparent to us.

1. Language learning and, therefore, language teaching must be integrated. Spelling problems are language problems.

2. The notion of stages in language and spelling development is not particularly useful, especially when it comes to meeting the needs of individual learners.

3. While conferring with children about their learning is vital, such conferences need positive direction. We need to develop teaching strategies to deal with specific problems.

1 Integration

Much has been written about integrating the various aspects of language, but there is some doubt as to how well this notion is understood. To many it means a thematic approach to language teaching, so that all language activities centre around a particular theme. However, while theme work may provide a vehicle for integration, it certainly does not guarantee it. We are indebted to the work of Carolyn Burke, which enabled us to articulate what it was that our class was demonstrating to us. Burke (see Harste, Woodward and Burke 1984) used the concept of the Linguistic Data Pool to help explain how language is developed.

As we have suggested, language is learned in use, and so every encounter with language provides a demonstration of language and the way it is used. The Linguistic Data Pool represents the language information possessed by a person and developed through various encounters with language. It is this pool of information which we draw on in subsequent language encounters, as the following diagram illustrates.

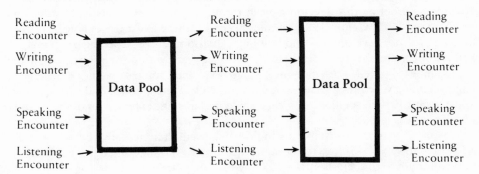

The notion of the Linguistic Data Pool suggests that statements that we learn to write by writing and to read by reading are far too simplistic. True, if children are to read and write, they must have encounters with reading and writing, but what they know about oral language is equally important. There is as much to be learned about writing from reading and talking as there is from writing itself. In fact it is impossible to develop as a writer unless you are a reader.

With spelling, our aim is that children become standard spellers. Where is standard spelling demonstrated? It is principally through our reading that we learn standard spelling, yet many of us can point to people who are avid readers but poor standard spellers. There must be something about the way good spellers read. We call it reading with a writer's perception and you can only do this if you are a writer. At this stage we can only speculate about what this writer's perception is, but it obviously includes some kind of sensitivity to words in both oral and written contexts.

We found the notion of the Linguistic Data Pool very liberating from a teaching point of view. Although we had timetabled a block of language study, we were concerned that the children still had time clearly labelled as oral language, reading and writing. They demonstrated that these were *our* concerns and that they did not make such distinctions. One had only to watch them at their writing to see that a lot of talk and reading was going on too. Although we continued to encourage a variety of language activities, we became much less concerned if we spent most of the language period caught up in a reading activity that the children were clearly enjoying, because we were confident that they were learning about writing. Similarly, the next day might be spent concentrating on writing. Since many reading activities involved writing and vice versa, and both a great deal of talk, we were also confident that the children were getting plenty of language each day. We believe that this integration of language activities is crucial to the development of oral and written language (which of course includes spelling). It is through such integration that children become sensitive to the language demonstrations which surround them.

2 Stages to strategies

Before you can help children with any aspect of their language development, you must make some assessment of their language needs. It is easy enough to identify the non-standard, but how do you move children towards the standard? Children in classrooms all over Australia have clearly demonstrated that spelling, like other aspects of language learning, is developmental, and a number of researchers have attempted to define this development in terms of stages (see Beers & Henderson 1977; Zutell 1979; Gentry 1981). While this had seemed like a reasonable basis for assessing learner development and building classroom writing/spelling programs, it had also become obvious, even before we began work with our class, that such an approach was limited. For while these stages explained some of what we observed children doing when they wrote, there was much left unexplained and often highly idiosyncratic in their spelling. However, since the language experiences of each child differ, this was not surprising.

We found it more profitable to look at what children actually did when they attempted to spell. This lead to the identification of a number of language strategies that children use to spell (Bouffler 1983), which may be set out as follows.

Spelling as it sounds

This refers to what is generally known as phonetic spelling and is based on the assumption of a direct sound/symbol relationship. The use of letter names is part of this strategy.

STASHON—station   CUZENZ—cousins   DA—day

Spelling as it sounds out

This is similar to the previous strategy except that it involves a sounding-out procedure which causes sounds to be exaggerated, so that phonetic features not normally represented in spelling are identified.

HUW—who   The release of the vowel is heard and represented.
HAFH—half

Evidence suggests that this strategy is more likely to be used by an immature speller.

Spelling as it articulates

This makes use of the articulatory aspects of sound, particularly place and manner of articulation.

BRIF—brief   The vowels involved are close in place of articulation.
CHRIDAGEN—tried again   'T' and 'ch' are close in place of articulation.

Those familiar with the work of Charles Read (1975) will recognise that this strategy encompasses many of the features of children's early spelling which he identified.

Spelling as it means

Here semantic units are represented.

WASUPONATIM—Once upon a time
HAVTO—have to
REFRIDGERATORED—refridgerated

This principle underlies much standard spelling, e.g. nation/nationality; sign/signal.

Spelling as it looks

As the name suggests, this is a visual strategy which uses graphic patterning rather than sound/symbol relationships. To some degree it is involved in all spelling.

SHCOOL—school   WITHE—white   YUO—you

Spelling by analogy

This strategy is based on the principle that what you learn in one situation can apply in another.

REALISTICK—realistic   RESKYOU—rescue   SHO—shoe

Spelling by linguistic context

The spelling of a word may be influenced by the linguistic environment in which it occurs: e.g. 'any' written under the word *envelope* becomes 'ENY'.

Spelling by reference to an authority

When you do not know you can ask someone, find the word in a printed text or look in the dictionary.

Opting for an alternative structure

When in doubt, use another word. Children may simply settle for one vowel to use in all cases of doubt.

Spelling by being indeterminate

This strategy is used with handwritten text. The writer throws the onus on the reader to decide: e.g. is it 'ei' or 'ie'? Put the dot in the middle and make the 'i' and 'e' look similar!

One or several of these strategies may be involved in the spelling of any one word in a text. It is, however, impossible to say what combination of strategies produces standard spelling, partly because it is possible to spell words in more than one way and still obey the rules of English orthography. With the exception perhaps of sounding-out, adults also use these strategies when faced with a word they do not know. Invented spelling is not a stage but a strategy used by all writers. Because adults have a greater pool of language data to draw on, their use of one or other of these strategies is, in general, more likely to produce standard forms.

These strategies can be useful in guiding children, as we found when conferring with our children about their spelling. If they were stuck with a word, we would direct them to the most appropriate strategy or strategies. Sometimes these were sound/symbol strategies, at other times meaning or visual strategies, or analogy—even combinations of these. It is important that children develop a range of strategies, for though spelling problems are complex, it is obvious that over-reliance on one or other strategy is likely to inhibit spelling development.

3 Developing teaching strategies

Although the identification of spelling strategies assisted us when conferring with children about spelling, we still felt that somehow there was a lack of direction in what we were doing. However, this was a general problem with writing and not specifically confined to spelling. Some children seemed to have so many problems that we did not know where to start with them. This is when we first began to appreciate that some of our writers were not in control of what they were doing, and that we needed to give them control by developing specific teaching strategies to deal with their problems. We needed to support them in the process of their writing, rather than let them fall in a heap and then try to put them together during conferences. To put it another way, children often need more support than we can provide for them through a conference.

With small classes it is possible to teach through individual or group conferences, but we found that it was much more difficult to give children the time they require when confronted with larger groups. We worked hard on our conference technique to avoid being nothing more than verbal red pens, but we were still not satisfied that these conferences gave sufficient support, direction and control to the learner.

Chrystine Bouffler clarifies a point.

By returning to our simple diagram of the writing cycle you can see how we began to solve this problem. In it we have identified aspects of the writing process—focusing, composing, editing and proofreading. By developing teaching strategies which focus on one or other of these aspects, as needed, we can support writing development. In short, we looked for strategies to get writing started, to assist in

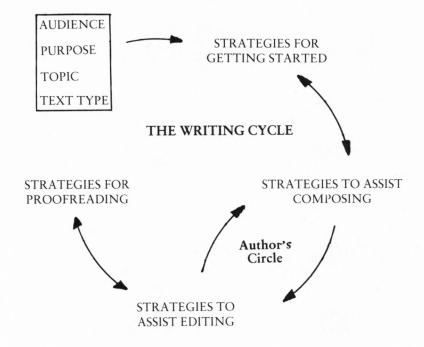

AUDIENCE

PURPOSE

TOPIC

TEXT TYPE

STRATEGIES FOR
GETTING STARTED

THE WRITING CYCLE

STRATEGIES FOR
PROOFREADING

STRATEGIES TO ASSIST
COMPOSING

**Author's
Circle**

STRATEGIES TO
ASSIST EDITING

composing (more often than not these were reading activities), to focus on editing and to encourage proofreading.

Some of these strategies were individual, while others involved the whole class. Sometimes they constrained the children's writing so as to focus on a particular aspect of the process, although the children seldom, if ever, saw them as constraints—especially when they achieved a degree of success. For example, we encouraged some of our more reluctant young writers, who were loath to take risks with their writing, to compose their versions of predictable books. This obviously constrains the writing, but the predictable structure supports the writer and guarantees a degree of success—and nothing succeeds like success. The conference then becomes more manageable because there is less to confer about.

We have argued that spelling does not stand apart from writing and reading. To understand how we go about assisting learners with spelling, it's necessary to have some understanding of our writing and reading program. To attempt to discuss spelling separately would be self-defeating. Accordingly, some of the teaching strategies which we share in the following chapters do not explicitly affect spelling. However, since they bear on the development of written language in general, we would argue that they implicitly affect spelling. There are still those who believe that you do not teach spelling unless you give children lists of words to learn, or unless you label specific teaching strategies spelling. Because of this we have endeavoured to highlight the connections between our teaching strategies and spelling development, where such connections can be shown.

Chapter Three

CREATING CONTEXT

Since writing does not occur in a vacuum, the first step in establishing a writing program is to create contexts for writing in your classroom. For many young children the mere act of creating a written message is reason enough to write. Initially they want to create messages and to share them with other members of the class. However, this initial impetus must be maintained and directed if children are to develop as writers, and for this to happen they need contexts which give their writing direction and purpose. Sometimes 'school' reasons are appropriate, but if the only reason a child ever writes is because the teacher demands it, writing will soon become a chore. Like so many before them, children will lose interest and write only when they have no choice but to do so.

When creating contexts for writing it is important to bear the following points in mind:

- Children need an environment filled with written language.
- Children need audiences for their writing.
- Children need to be able to write for different purposes.
- Children need to be able to write on a variety of topics. This is closely related to the type of texts they write. Some topics are more appropriate to one type of text than another.
- Children need to be able to write different types of text. Story has its place, but it is only one of the many types of text children write.

The context for writing is also extremely important for the development of spelling, especially standard spelling. There is a great deal of evidence to suggest that where learners perceive the context to be relevant and one that demands standard spelling, they are likely to show a greater concern for standard spelling. Nobody illustrates this better than Ron.

Occasionally our work brings us into contact with high schools. Ron was in the bottom group of a Year 8. Like so many others, he had learned to cope with failure by insulating himself behind a wall of academic indifference and bravado. His

English teacher had interested the group in writing stories for children in Grade 1 at the local primary school and had arranged for them to read their stories to the Grade 1 children. Somewhat surprisingly Ron showed a mild interest in the project. He wrote and shared a story. Then as a consequence of the sharing, Ron's group decided to turn the stories into illustrated books which would be put in the Grade 1 class library. Suddenly the dictionary became Ron's constant companion and he began to ask for help with spelling. When asked why it was suddenly so important, he replied, 'Well you can't have them little kids seeing bad spelling, can you?' For Ron this was a situation that demanded standard spelling and he responded to it. There are many reasons why people like Ron fail at school, but it was obvious that he had never really seen writing as a worthwhile activity and consequently was not concerned with standard spelling until he wrote for the 'little kids'.

Environments

To develop as users of written language children need to be surrounded by written language. While it is true that the day-to-day environment may expose them to plenty of it, it must be remembered that they spend a large portion of their day in school, and so it's important that print environments be created in the classroom. Harste, Woodward and Burke (1984) have clearly demonstrated how children respond to the print in their environment. They were also able to show that children's early attempts at writing reflect their culture. English-speaking children produce English-like shapes, Arabic children's attempts look like Arabic, and so on. Young writers

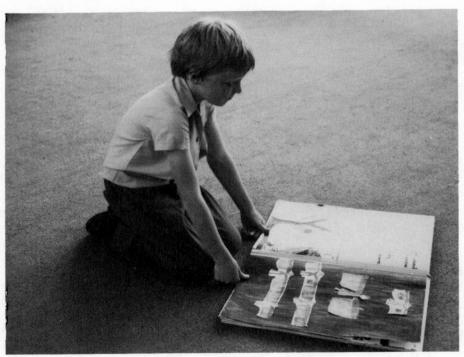

A quiet moment with a class book.

scrounge from their environment to help them create their written texts. They will go to print around the room, to books they have read or to previous stories they have written to assist them with letters or words they need. It is crucial, therefore, that such print be readily available in the classroom.

Audience

By tradition, the most common audience for children's writing is the classroom teacher. It has been extended to include classroom peers, but even this becomes narrow and restricting. Children need to go beyond the immediate classroom if they are to learn the importance of making meaning clear and of standard grammar and spelling. On many occasions the teacher will have to select audiences, but these should be as 'natural' as possible. Finding audiences outside the classroom is a test of ingenuity: here are some that we have used.

Writing messages—to each other, members of other classes, reminders to take home, etc.

Letters—to request information, to correspond with pen-friends or absent classmates, to enter competitions of all kinds, to respond to experiences, such as plays, etc.

Labels—to attach to class displays, to provide direction in the classroom, etc.

Signs to advertise coming school or class events, to support fund-raising ventures.

Newsletters—for parents and school members to keep them informed of class activities, including writing.

Magazines—class/school magazines for parents and peers.

Published stories—a class publishing company can be set up with editors, illustrators, etc. to produce books for the class/school library, to share with peers, other classes, senior citizens.

Plays—for class, school and parent groups.

Graffiti boards—for each other, to capture ideas and thoughts of members of the class and teachers.

Reports—for self or class on a variety of topics.

It is important that audiences respond as far as possible; i.e. that they reply to letters, react to stories, take action as requested, and so on.

Of all aspects of context audience appears to exert the greatest effect on children. Where children value their audience and are aware that it demands standard spelling, spelling assumes a greater importance. This was certainly true of the children in our class. Perhaps the clearest indication they gave us was when they wrote to the Queen to wish her a happy birthday. Even their initial composing showed less willingness to take risks with their spelling than they displayed when writing for other audiences. Clearly, they felt, a letter to such a person demands standard spelling.

Much has been written about publishing children's writing. We think the term 'publishing' is confusing because for most of us it has a well-developed and fairly precise meaning. The real issue is one of providing a broad range of audiences for children's writing, particularly audiences which demand the editing and proofreading of what has been written. While such audiences are to be found within the traditional area of publishing, they are not restricted to it. For instance, a letter of complaint to a company is not publishing in the traditional sense, but it assumes an audience that places certain demands on the writer. There is no doubt that book publishing is being overused in many classrooms—because the concept of audience has been narrowed by the concept of publishing in the minds of many teachers. Too much emphasis on book publishing trivialises it and leads to the publication of writing of dubious quality. Although it is to be hoped that some of the learners in our classrooms will become authors in the generally accepted sense of that word, and though children should have the experience of being classroom authors, the main aim of our writing program should be to turn children into writers and to help them enjoy their writing.

Purpose

It is almost impossible to talk of audience, or any aspect of context, without referring to the purpose of writing. Our list of potential audiences suggests particular purposes for writing. However, it is not unusual to find certain kinds of writing being made to serve purposes that have little to do with the purposes such writing serves in real life. Personal journals, for example, should be all that their name implies: places where one can engage in personal writing. Too often they become simply a teaching technique for dealing with surface features of language, such as standard spelling. Book publishing, as we have already suggested, is also in danger of becoming just another school literacy exercise, unless we consider what the purpose of such writing is.

   If children are to become competent writers, we must vary the audiences and purposes for writing. Risk taking is also a necessary ingredient for success, and so children need situations where they feel free to take risks with writing. They need time and encouragement to experiment, to draft and redraft. We found that this can sometimes put pressure on teachers when they are judged by what is produced. One of our young writers worked for a whole term on a single story, and there were times when we wondered whether we should encourage her to get moving. The calibre of the story she produced was, however, well worth the time taken, and we were glad we did not interfere. Another problem for teachers may arise when what are essentially first drafts are judged as finished products. (This is one reason why it is so important to have parents on side.)

   Early experimentation is crucial to the development of all language, and spelling is no exception. It is often said that if you allow children to 'invent' their own spelling when they begin writing, they will 'learn' non-standard forms. This argument suggests that language learning is a matter of habit. But if language is context specific, it can never be a matter of habit—nor can language learning. It is rather a matter of discovering how language is used by using it and having chances to experiment with it. It's by experimenting that children learn the strategies necessary to produce English spelling (those strategies listed in the previous chapter). They also learn the parameters of English phonology: what kinds of spelling English allows and does not allow. While this knowledge does not necessarily produce standard spelling, it is crucial to spelling development because it is the kind of knowledge which releases the writer from the constraints of memory. You have to know the possible spellings of a word when you are uncertain of the standard spelling, as otherwise you cannot use a dictionary to check. In fact, one of the hardest spelling problems to deal with is the child who has not developed a repertoire of possible spellings and the spelling strategies that produce them.

We have suggested that children need audiences and purposes which demand standard spelling and that children should be encouraged to take risks. However, in our experience some audiences may reduce a child's willingness to take risks with spelling. Encouraging children to draft, where appropriate, certainly gives them the opportunity to risk take, but not surprisingly this too is affected by the audience and purpose. Our letters to the Queen were drafted, but the restraint was obvious even at draft stage. The children stuck to what they knew they could spell or could find out without too much difficulty. Although their caution was understandable, it does emphasise the importance of varying the audience and purpose.

When we started on our program we thought that the concepts of audience and purpose were beyond the grasp of the neophyte writer. What we failed to realise was that this attitude violated our beliefs about writing. If nobody can write in a vacuum, and audience and purpose are part of the context for writing, then children—even very young children—must respond to these elements of context. Our class clearly demonstrated this to us, and while some children were still struggling with their writing, they found the task easier to cope with when they knew why they were writing and who would read it.

Topic

Writing contexts more often than not create their own topics. If the purpose of the writing is to invite someone into the classroom, then the topic is clear. If the writing results, for example, from a classroom literature activity or a science activity, the topic will be suggested by the activity. There are other situations where the topic is not necessarily dictated by the writing context—in story writing, for instance—and then it's important that children have the opportunity to select their own topics. Once this is realised, the question of whether or not to set a topic ceases to be an issue.

It is a widely accepted notion that we can all write more easily about things we know or have experienced, and so it's important to create writing contexts where this is possible. It is also true that some children need help to discover those areas in which they are 'experts'. On the other hand, writing helps us to discover what we do not know or what we need to know, and it's equally important that children have opportunities to break new ground. At such times the teacher may take a more active role in directing topic choice by specifying the general topic area, or even the specific topic. This is very often necessary with writing in the Science and Social Science areas. Indeed, as children enter high school, the need to be able to write on specified topics becomes greater. There are good arguments for wishing to see this trend changed, but the realities of assessment suggest that we should not ignore it.

The effects of topic on spelling are less obvious, and since the various aspects of context are closely interrelated, it's probably somewhat artificial to break them up in this way. Nevertheless it helps our understanding. Clearly the scope of our spelling is the range of topics we explore through writing, reading and talking. The more tenuous our command of the topic, and the more we have to struggle with it, the more likely we are to produce non-standard spellings in our writing, because most of our attention is taken up with the topic. Conversely, it's likely that those topics over which we have control, or seek to develop control, are areas of our reading, and so we are more exposed to the standard form of words related to such topics.

Text types

Particularly in the early grades, there is a tendency for teachers to view all written messages as story. It is not uncommon to hear both teachers and children refer to early writing attempts as stories. This is not only a possible source of confusion but one reason why so many process writing programs lack a sense of direction. Narrative structure is well established in our society. Ask any layman and you will be told that a story has a beginning, a middle and an end. Just what this means we will discuss presently. The point about this structure is that, while there may be variations, most story in our society follows this basic pattern. When children first start to write they naturally find it easier to recount or comment on personal experiences. Story makes too many cognitive demands. What they produce, far from being immature stories, are other types of text which themselves need nurturing and developing. The story form develops as children become readers of stories.

In developing reading/writing programs teachers need to recognise different types of text, consider the purposes for which they are usually used by writers, and set up contexts in the classroom which allow for their development. There is a school of thought which suggests that children should be taught different kinds of text structure. However, our experience suggests that children come to an understanding of different kinds of text by having a need to make use of them and by being exposed to them through reading. In other words they learn to differentiate them in the same way as they learn to differentiate other language categories. In the early stages of talking all men may be 'Daddy' until the child learns to differentiate. Similarly all text may be story until the child learns otherwise. But we cannot expect children to learn the difference when, as teachers, we are confused.

In making judgements about writing the characteristics of particular types of text are important considerations. If the context demands story, then our judgements and the help we offer the writer should be in terms of story. A simple comment cannot be judged by the same criteria that we apply to story or vice versa. It often happens that children who are attempting more complicated forms of text are seen as less able writers than those who have control over less complex text types. Judgements are still made on the basis of surface language, and not on the basis of what the child is trying to achieve in the text.

Exploring different types of text is beyond the scope of this book, but it may be of help to identify the different kinds of text that young children tend to write. Here we are indebted to the work of Martin & Rothery (1984). Classifications are by no means exhaustive and other types of classification are possible, but we have found these useful in our work.

Writing across the curriculum—gathering information.

Observation/Comment

In this kind of text the child writes about an experience and comments on that experience. The observations and comments do not follow any order except that established by the writer. John's comments on his first day at school illustrate this.

> *My first day at school I was nervous becouse I didn't no what it was going to be like at school. At the other school the rooms were mutch moor smaller than this class room bacouse at the other school there wasn't that much people there. I like being in this class because I will get moor freinds. This class room has got a t.v. I like watching it.*

> *My first day at school . . . . much people there.* . . . .   Observation
> *I like being in this class . . . moor freinds.* . . . .   Comment
> *This class room has got a t.v.* . . . .   Observation
> *I like watching it.* . . . .   Comment

Recount

In this type of text children recount experiences. There is usually a setting of some kind followed by a series of temporally sequenced events, which may conclude with some kind of reorientation in time or space. The following is John's recount of a day at school.

*Yesterday it was Aboriganal day and we all made dampa first then my group
went to see the dance. There were 4 dances after that we went to the film and
talk with the man and after that we went to painting finerly we ate the dampa
and fish and we went home.*

Yesterday it was Aboriganal day.	Orientation
and we all made dampa first	Event
then my group went to see the dance.	Event
There were 4 dances	Event
after that we went to the film and talk with the man	Event
and after that we went to painting	Event
finerly we ate the dampa and fish and we went home.	Reorientation or Conclusion

Narrative

For most people narrative has a beginning, a middle and an end. This is another way
of saying that it begins with some kind of temporal or spatial setting, is then followed
by a complication or series of complications—things do not go as they should or
something unexpected happens—and, finally, the complications are in some way
resolved. There may even be a series of complications and resolutions before the final
one. Penny's text has all the elements of narrative or story.

*There was a dictionary once near a fruit bowl but no one ever used it. It was
so sad that it cried words. One day it started to yell out words because it got
tired of sitting doing nothing. The people who lived in the house came out of
their bedrooms and said, 'What is all this racket?' and they looked around.*

*The people said, 'STOP YELLING' but the dictionary didn't stop yelling.
The dictionary only kept on talking. It said all sorts of things like 'Hello,
goodbye, biscuit, bicycle and blanket', it never stopped.*

*'We will have to get rid of that dictionary' said Mrs. Jones, she is the mother
who lives in the house.*

*So they did do something about the dictionary. They put a rock on it. It
started talking about rocks, all the things about rocks. They took the rock off
the dictionary and took it out to the bin and put it in. You could still hear it, it
was talking about how people drop litter all over the place.*

*The people in the family said they would give up but they didn't. So they put
the dictionary on the plane and the plane flew to Spain. He was GONE!*

There was a dictionary once near a fruit bowl.	Orientation
It was lonely so it began to talk. This annoyed the people in the house. They put a rock on it. It didn't work. They put it in the bin. It still kept talking. They put it on a plane.	Series of Complications
The plane flew to Spain. The dictionary was gone.	Resolution

Report

This type of text usually deals with factual information of some kind. It may be a description of something experienced or a report of facts gathered. The writer is distanced from the subject and does not comment on personal involvement. Reports usually contain generalisation, description, classification and/or explanation. David's report on dinosaurs may help to illustrate this.

> *Dianorsars lived many years ago. Over the years they vanished. The Terenasores Rex was the terriblest dianorsor of the lot. There were thousands of dianorsores here are some Brontasoros Stegasoras. Most of them are bad. People have found bones from them. Some live in water. The big ones stay on dry land.*

Dianorsars lived . . . . they vanished.	Generalisation
Terenasores Rex . . . of the lot.	Classification
There were thousands of dianorsores	Generalisation
Here are some . . . Stegasoras	Classification
Most of them are bad.	Description/Generalisation
People have found bones from them.	Explanation
Some live . . . on dry land.	Description

A much fuller explanation of text types is given by Frances Christie (1986). Although she refers to them as text genres, we have avoided using this term because of confusion about its meaning in educational literature.

Varying the shape of context

Once writers have a sense of their Topic, Audience, Purpose and the Type of Text they want to write, they are in a position to start their writing. This is not to say that each of these aspects of context is necessarily delineated clearly before writing starts. Sometimes one or other may be unclear when we start but is clarified as we write. Without a sense of context, however, we could not write. In our experience writing is generally easier when you have a clear sense of audience and purpose, know your topic and know how to construct the kind of text you wish to write. Those who never find writing 'easy' may well take issue with this, but we believe it holds as a general principle.

Context is what makes each language experience unique. It is not something that can be packaged and sold as a language scheme. Reading, writing and spelling schemes that centre around particular subjects or themes are just that. They are not language in context, although some make out that they are. How you use them may well place them in a context, but only you can tell if it is the sort of context that stimulates language growth or inhibits it. To our way of thinking, any spelling scheme which presents lists, whether around a theme or not, begs the question of who is in control of the writing and the learning. Ideally the child is, but such lists yield little control even to the teacher.

Other subject areas can often provide excellent writing contexts, especially ones where you can develop a variety of text types. One of our more successful writing activities arose out of a Social Studies unit on leisure. The children, after some discussion, decided to invite people from the community to talk about unusual hobbies. Letters of invitation and thanks had to be written, and reports written and filed so that there would be a record of the talks. Many of the children were so enthused that they too prepared and researched their own presentations of particular interests and hobbies. Given the demands of writing in high school and beyond, it is imperative that we give more emphasis to writing in the subject areas than is generally given in primary schools.

Contexts not only shape understanding of the writing process, but the elements of context can provide direction for our language programs. We can create contexts that demand particular kinds of text and then set about developing children's command of those texts through a variety of reading, writing and oral language activities. This will perhaps become clearer as we discuss some of the teaching strategies we have used. There is some truth in the criticism that too much is left to chance in present approaches to writing, and our slower learners made us acutely aware of this. It took us some time, however, to fully realise that it is through creating and manipulating contexts that we can give direction to language activities for all language learners. If we wanted children to write letters, stories, reports, etc, we had to create the contexts in which such writing could take place. By manipulating context we could also give children opportunities to develop particular kinds of writing. Using context like this requires teachers to have an overall understanding of written language development and where they wish to take their children with writing. Unfortunately, however, writing development still proceeds in a haphazard fashion in some classrooms, even in those with a process-writing approach.

Chapter Four

GETTING STARTED

Children learn at a very early age that marks on a page can convey meaning. Before they come to school they are exposed to a vast range of written messages and most will have begun to experiment with creating their own messages. Some come to school able to write recognisable messages; others, although producing shapes that reflect written language, are not yet able to produce messages that are recognisable. There is also a small group of those who seem reluctant to commit pen to paper in any way, except perhaps by drawing. These children are generally the non-risk takers, and along with children who are slow to move into more conventional writing, pose a difficulty for the classroom teacher. We were not exempt from such difficulty. There were several children whose writing was slow to develop.

Getting started

Our first step in helping children to get started was to ensure that all who needed it had the alphabet in upper and lower case on their desks. We simply ran off the necessary stencils and attached them to the desks with clear Contact. This may seem rather trite, but traditionally such things have been around the room or on the blackboard, with the result that children often have to swivel around to find them, especially if they are not seated in traditional rows. They then have to find the letter they need and translate it to the page. This becomes time-consuming and disrupts the writing process, and it's not surprising that something sometimes gets lost in the translation. It is easier and much more efficient if the information learners need is on the desk in front of them.

Before we discuss specific strategies, it's worth noting that full details of strategies discussed in this and subsequent chapters will be found at the end of the chapters. As an alternative to traditional lesson plans we have provided Strategy Lesson Plans, which we hope teachers will use in their programs. Each lesson plan describes the rationale (i.e. the language concept which underpins it), the type of learner it is useful for, the materials needed and how the strategy operates. They show at a glance what you are doing with your class, why you are doing it and how it is done. We find them very powerful statements in terms of teacher accountability and they are also very useful for any relief teacher taking over your class. Traditional lesson programming is inappropriate because it reflects behaviourist notions of language and learning which are opposed to the views expressed in this book.

Written Conversation

Perhaps our most successful strategy for getting children started or moving on with their writing was *Written Conversation*, a strategy developed by Carolyn Burke. This is, as the name suggests, a conversation on paper. With young children we make something of a game of it. If you ask, those who cannot write will tell you that they can't. Ask them if they can pretend to write and most will have a go. Obviously the children who cannot read need some help to understand what you have written. But by controlling the conversation so that it does not demand too much from the child initially, you can even get the non-risk taker to have a go. The following brief conversation was the first with Gary. He was in first grade and could write his name and numbers up to 10, but spent most of the writing time drawing pictures. What he could do he did well, but he was a classical non-risk taker, not prepared to try anything he did not know he could do. His written language development was slow.

What is your name?

Gary

How old are you?

6

Do you have brothers and sisters?

ys

How many?

6

How many brothers?

ε

What do you like to play ?

†ɑℓℓ

Although this was a very one-sided conversation which initially required little from Gary, the last question tempted him and he had a go at spelling 'tackle'. A very small breakthrough, but a breakthrough nevertheless!

There are those children who are willing enough to try but just need some help to get going. Neville was such a case. He was an effervescent five-year-old who could write his own name and knew most of his letters. However, he did not have the strategies to put them together to produce the messages he wanted, and so helping him was a matter of directing him to the appropriate strategies. Since a very high percentage of English words are spelled as they sound, the first step is to direct children to that spelling strategy. With help Neville was then able to produce the following attempts at 'football' and 'everyday'.

What is your name ? NeVilk

How old are you ? 5

Do you like to play tackle ? fot dol

Do you play football on Saturday ? no

When do you play evriag

Do you play with your brothers ? yes

We do not allow children to become reliant on this spelling strategy. Once they get going, we start to direct them to other appropriate strategies, such as the look of words, their meaning and analogy.

Used in the way described above, Written Conversation is fairly labour-intensive and we do not suggest you do it every day with every child. We used it only with those children who needed it. We accepted what they wrote at other times and encouraged them. Because the written conversation actually gives more control to the learner, it gives the teacher more of a chance of supporting the learner. We consider it worth the time. It avoids that situation where you do not know where to start to help the child.

Written Conversation is not just a strategy for beginners; it can be used with reluctant writers of all ages. With older children the secret lies in being a good conversationalist. Children also enjoy conversations with each other. However, some difficulties can arise when children converse with each other, as a conversation 'overheard' by Christine Walsh shows. (Christine, a Victorian consultant and teacher, paid a number of visits to our class during the year, and more than once showed us the potential of things we were doing.) She observed the following conversation between Matthew and Alexander and used the writing situation to turn the conversation around. Matthew accused Alexander of having mucus in his eyes. To Alexander's way of thinking Matthew was fat and maggoty. The boys were left in no doubt about Christine's reaction and immediately amended their behaviour. And not a word was spoken!

your 4 eye have muse in all
that heard you are fat and magt on
Who wants to talk if they are
horrible to each other?
No one!
And it can't be helped if we
are fat or skinny, have glasses or
wooden legs.
We are still nice people inside!
SO
FORGET IT AND START AGAIN!
RIGHT?

Matthew + Alexander
well at chismas mum droped the pavlover and
we all lafed but mum did not louf it was all
over her she did not like it was all right

Did mum make another Pavlova? Or
did she doo something else? No she up to the
pavlover and did another pavlover
Well my mum wasted 24 eggs on 1
pavlova for my birthday party!
well that all right every one make mistake
Yeh! I make lots of mistakes. Do you?
yes I do make mistakes
you have a good bike but the wills are buded
buy the way I crach your bik yestday

Christine also has an interesting variation of Written Conversation. Using an overhead projector she conducts conversations with the class which provide a forum for developing logical thinking. Her conversation might begin with something like, 'I have a pet. I bet you can't guess what kind of pet it is.' The children take it in turns to write their answers, sometimes with help from her. Of course the tendency is to guess at random, and so she uses the conversation to show them how to find the right answer.

Predictable Books

There is little point in learning to spell unless you write. Since writing encompasses spelling, any strategy that gets children writing gives them a chance of learning to become standard spellers. The trouble with so many poor spellers is that they are also reluctant writers. Some argue that if we teach them to spell, they will be able to write and therefore more willing to. This argument is tantalisingly simplistic because it totally ignores the complex relationship of reading and writing and the role of spelling. You cannot hope to tackle spelling until you get children writing. Another useful strategy to get children writing is *Predictable Books*.

Predictable books have been used to assist beginning readers. They utilise highly predictable but meaningful text, often exploiting accumulation (as in *I Know an Old Lady*, Ashton Scholastic, 1985) or repetition of ideas (as in *Brown Bear*, Rigby, 1985) or combinations of these. Rhyme may add to the predictability and changes in the text can be signalled by appropriate pictures. Just as such books can be used to assist beginning readers, so they can be used to provide young writers with a supportive structure on which to base their own versions. The story-line is there for them to use and by going back to the original, i.e. by approaching the book as writers, they can get help with their spelling, although the need to provide their own alternative also encourages some creativity and risk-taking with spelling.

One child in our group benefited particularly from this strategy, and because he provided the greatest challenge to our approach, it is worth saying more about him.

Ben

Ben was in Year 2 and was almost eight years old before he began to write. In writing time he had learned to model the behaviour of other children and sat quietly making strokes and circles across the page from right to left. Over time he became more and more dissatisfied with his writing attempts; nevertheless his behaviour remained consistent. On most occasions he was willing to 'tell' his story to others. After four years in the lower school Ben had learned he was a failure. He was unwilling to take risks and would not attempt any writing other than the strokes and circles because he knew it would be wrong. Any efforts he did make were positively reinforced, but Ben was in real danger of being labelled a slow learner.

While we were concerned with Ben's lack of progress in all areas of language, the most immediate problem was his very poor self-concept. We worked on this in class, and meetings were arranged with Ben's parents to seek their support at home. It took time, but gradually Ben became more confident and began to use letter shapes to convey his message. During the second half of the year student teachers visited the school to work individually with children. We took the opportunity to give Ben an extra hour of language work each week. Under supervision, a student devised and implemented a program of reading and writing with him. Two factors shaped this program. Firstly, Ben had never had a book published, which was of some concern to him although we placed little emphasis on such publishing, and, secondly, his writing was hampered by the fact that he was unsure of letter names. To address both these problems the student worked with him to produce a predictable alphabet book based on *Q is for Duck* (Houghton Mifflin/Clarion, 1980). The structure is quite simple—A is for Zoo. Why? Because Animals live in a Zoo. This proved to be the turning point for Ben. The notions in the book appealed to him and provided an unthreatening model for his writing.

Although Ben's progress from this point was not spectacular, it was steady. The next year he progressed into Year 3 and in March wrote the following letter:

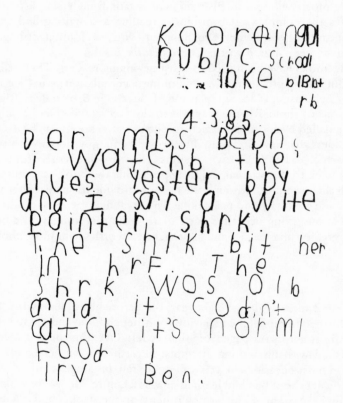

Dear Miss Bean,
I watched the news yesterday and I saw a white pointer shark. The shark bit her in half. The shark was old and couldn't catch its normal food.
Love Ben

There is little doubt that Ben has some way to go, but this letter is a far cry from the circles and strokes he was producing mid-way through Year 2. It shows that he has developed some strategies for producing spellings—in particular spelling as it sounds, including the use of letter names. Although he is having some difficulty in representing vowels, his strategies are meeting with a degree of success since it's possible to read his message. The fact that some of his spelling is standard would also suggest that he is more sensitive to the written language that surrounds him. With children like Ben it is very easy to allow the surface features of their writing to obscure their success.

Several other strategies which fall into the 'getting started' category are worth mentioning, although they are not explicitly related to spelling.

Picture Writing

There is nothing new about using pictures as an impetus for writing, but we have found it an excellent strategy for helping children through those periods where inspiration for writing seems to dry up. It's also an excellent strategy for encouraging story writing. Carolyn Burke's variations of this old technique provide greater support for the learner than does simply asking the child to write about the picture. The strategy is described at the end of this chapter, but the secret lies in the choice of pictures. These should be background pictures, devoid of characters, so that the learner has to create and draw them. The drawing acts as a way of focusing or, as Murray would call it, rehearsing, and by the time the learner has developed and drawn the characters, a story has started to emerge. This approach also prevents the learner from simply writing about the picture. We found that once we showed the children what to do, they took control. We kept a box of pictures on hand, covered with clear Contact or laminated for durability. Children would make use of them when they felt the need. Whenever we wished to assist particular learners with story writing, however, it was necessary to be more directive in our approach, though the choice of picture was still up to the learner.

Bundling

Once again, this is not a new strategy, but it is useful for assisting learners with non-narrative text, and for teaching paragraphing. It requires a supply of small pieces of paper and so it's a good way of using up old computer printouts and the like. Learners record what they know about their subjects, putting one piece of information on each piece of paper, which can then be arranged to give direction to writing. This is not the same as drawing up the plan of a piece of writing, but rather a way of focusing and organising. Should the writing take another direction, the pieces can be rearranged or thrown away as necessary. The strategy reveals gaps in information and is one way of avoiding the wholesale plagiarism that school projects so often encourage. Most children enjoy projects, but unfortunately they often fall short of being the valuable learning experiences they should be. The key to academic success is not copying out large chunks of information, but being able to take information and make it your own.

STRATEGY LESSON PLANS

These strategies are suitable for all age groups. They worked well with children in our class and we have used them equally successfully with older learners.

Written Conversation

Rationale
Each encounter we have with language may increase our knowledge of language and the way it is used. We can make use of this knowledge in subsequent language encounters, and so knowledge of oral language can be used to assist in the development of written language. Written Conversation makes use of the give and take and immediate feedback of oral language to support and encourage written language. It is non-threatening because the emphasis is on the message, not on the surface features of language. It requires the learner to take risks with spelling and thus encourages the development of spelling strategies.

Learner suitability
This strategy is useful for learners who are reluctant to write and those who are loath to take risks with spelling. It may also be used with any learner to encourage logical thinking.

Materials required
Pen and paper, or, if done as a class activity, an O.H. projector.

Procedure
Two participants converse on paper. They are usually the teacher and the learner but may be two learners. The teacher may also 'converse' with the class using an O.H. projector. Young children who say they cannot write can be encouraged to pretend to write. In cases where the learner has not developed as a reader, the teacher may need to help by reading what is written.

Predictable Books

Rationale
Reading is a process of sampling print, predicting meaning and confirming/correcting on the basis of further sampling. The more predictable the meaning is, the easier a text is to read. Learners can be assisted to read by the creation of highly predictable texts. Such texts can also be used to support early attempts at writing by requiring learners to model writing on particular patterns. This draws the learners' attention to spelling, while the element of improvisation also allows them to develop and test their spelling strategies.

Learner suitability
This strategy is suitable for all learners, but particularly for those who are slow to develop reading and writing and reluctant to take risks.

Materials required
A collection of books with highly predictable story-lines. Predictability is enhanced

by the repetition of an idea (as in *Q is for Duck*), by accumulation (as in *I Know an Old Lady*), by rhyme, by pictures that signal changes in the text, and by combinations of these.

Procedure
Read and enjoy the book. Encourage the learners to use the predictable pattern of the book to create their own versions.

Picture Writing

Rationale
When we write, we start with an idea of what we will write about, and during the writing process this idea becomes clarified and refined. Pictures provide a focus for writing. All narrative has setting and characters, and by providing the setting and encouraging the writer to create the characters, we can encourage learners to develop narrative writing. Drawing also serves to focus ideas.

Learner suitability
This strategy is suitable for all learners once they begin to write with confidence. It is particularly useful for developing story writing.

Materials required
A collection of pictures, preferably laminated or covered with clear Contact. They should have no human characters, so that they serve only as a setting for a possible story. Old calendars are a good source.

Procedure
The learner chooses a picture and then creates and draws characters to go with it. Initially children may require some help to do this. Cut out the drawings and stick them onto the picture. The writer now has sufficient information to commence writing. Developing the characters helps to create the story.

Bundling

Rationale
All text has structure. How it is structured depends upon the kind of text it is and the information the writer wishes to convey. Organising this information can assist the writer to focus and structure a written text.

Learner suitability
This strategy is suitable for all writers, especially those who need help in structuring factual, non-narrative text. It is also particularly useful for teaching paragraphing.

Materials required
A supply of cards or paper of uniform size, approximately 8 x 6 cm.

Procedure
Have learners jot down all that they know about their chosen and/or researched topic, recording each fact or piece of information on a separate card. Then help them to select the main ideas from the cards, and group or 'bundle' the remaining cards under these main ideas, as shown overleaf.

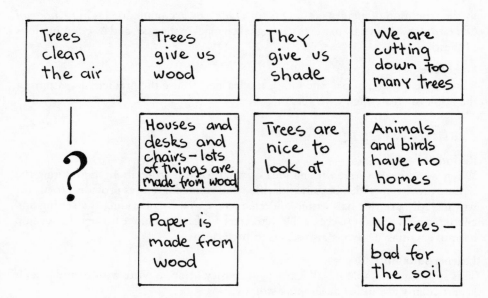

The organisation can then be used as a basis for writing. The information can be added to, subtracted from, and reorganised during writing, but the bundles provide focus and initial structure to support the writer during the process.

These strategies are by no means exhaustive; they are simply ones that we found useful. It would be limiting to consider them only as 'getting started' strategies, as all of them not only get learners started but support them through the process by providing a framework in which they can operate with some success.

Such strategies are not designed to replace the teacher/learner interaction which should go on in the classroom, but to supplement it. Conferencing still had a place in our classroom, although there was a subtle change in its nature because the children were enjoying some success with their writing.

Chapter Five

COMPOSING: THE READING/WRITING CONNECTION

Once the children got started with their writing we faced the question of how to help them with their composing. This was not simply a matter of developing a set of strategies; it also meant addressing the broader and more complex issue of maintaining and giving direction to the initial writing impetus. Our experiences, both with our K-2 class and with subsequent classes and their teachers, suggest that the broader issues have to be faced before you can develop successful teaching strategies. Your strategies depend largely on your solution to the larger problem.

Contexts

Several factors seem to be involved in maintaining and developing writing. The first of these—providing appropriate contexts—we have already discussed in Chapter 3. Talking with children about their perceptions of writing can often be a very enlightening experience. Not surprisingly, however, there is one message that comes through loud and clear: children consider purposeless writing activities a waste of time, and why not! Even in classrooms that embody the principles of 'process writing', children can become very disillusioned if writing has no audience or purpose and if it tends to be all of the same kind. The following conversation with Karen, a fifth-grader, is very revealing.

C.B: (*pointing to a large collection of published books displayed in a corner of the classroom*) Have you published a book?

K: Just one.

C.B: Would you like to show it to me?

K: Yeah, um, I guess so. (*She identifies her book.*)

C.B: How many books have the others had published?

K: Most of them have three or four.

C.B: Don't you like publishing books? You seem like a good writer.

K: Oh, it's okay, I suppose . . . (*pause*) I don't like stories. Stories are boring.

C.B: What do you mean stories are boring? Can you explain it to me? Don't you like to read stories?

K: Oh yeah! I read a lot but I don't like writing stories.

C.B: Why not?

K: I dunno.

C.B: Don't you like writing or is it just stories you don't like?

K: Yeah, um, I think writing is okay. I like projects. I'm doing one on gold. (*Here we launched into a discussion about gold . . . .*)

C.B: I'm still interested in why you don't like stories, especially if you enjoy reading them. Can you tell me any more about it?

K: I dunno. All we do most of the time in writing is write stories. We choose our own topics and things but it gets boring.

C.B: Why?

K: (*after some hesitation*) It's all the same. Who reads them anyway?

C.B: Do you find stories hard to write?

K: I suppose so. I'm, um, not very good at it.

Perhaps Karen would not have found story writing so boring if she had been better at it. If the published stories were any indication, there were others in the class who would have benefited from some more structured help with story writing. Karen's comment about reading them suggests that, for her at least, story writing was a purposeless activity. Discussions with other children in Karen's class also suggested that the writing program was becoming 'stale' because it lacked audience, other than classmates, and purpose.

Models

Children need two kinds of models if they are to be convinced of the value of writing and develop as writers. They need to see people writing, and they need to be exposed to a variety of written language forms. And if talking to children about writing is enlightening, talking to teachers is equally so. Of the teachers with whom we come into contact in the course of our work, we estimate that over 75% do not perceive themselves as good writers and do not enjoy writing. At this point we can only speculate as to why this is so, but it certainly poses problems for those who are teachers of writing. Most of us tend to avoid things we do not enjoy and are not particularly good at, and teachers are no exception. But it is difficult, if not impossible, to enthuse a class if you are not enthusiastic yourself.

Teachers who do not enjoy writing and are not particularly good at it are unlikely to write with their class. Children may see things written on the board, duplicated sheets, letters home, etc, but these, together with the books and other material they read, are the *products* of the writing process. Unless children come from families where a great deal of writing takes place, they seldom see demonstrations of the process itself. On the other hand, most K-6 teachers read to and with their classes, demonstrating the value of reading, if not the process.

What this difference between writing and reading demonstrates to children about literacy is hard to say. Some children certainly develop some dysfunctional notions about it. One of the most common is that good writers—and good readers—don't make mistakes. Even as we encourage children to draft and redraft, they see it as something they have to do to become good writers and not something that is part of the process. As six-year-old Adam put it, 'I want to be a good writer so that I don't have to write everything more than once.' It's certainly true that many of our generation, although we may be avid readers, are fairly ambivalent about writing.

We have come to realise that one of the weaknesses in our K-2 program was that we did not share our writing process enough. Gollasch (1986) has developed an interesting technique of demonstrating writing in process by using the board or O.H. projector, or more recently a word processor, to write himself. He asks the class to help him find a topic and then he writes on that topic, thinking aloud as he goes. He invites the class to read aloud what he has written and to make constructive criticisms. It's not easy to do this if your concept of yourself as a writer is poor, but you do not have to be a good writer. You can turn your 'weaknesses' to advantage by enlisting the help of the children. Children not only learn that all writers have their difficulties, but the learning becomes more of a co-operative venture. The children enjoy it and it encourages positive attitudes to writing and learning.

One of the problems of writing with children is finding the time to do it. Although you can sometimes compose on the board, you also need to share your writing on occasions when members of the class are also sharing, e.g. during group conferences. We have found it useful to have 5–10 minutes of U.S.S.W.—Uninterrupted Sustained Silent Writing. This has two advantages. It gives you time to write and it throws the children back on their own resources. They cannot ask questions during this time because you are writing, and so they have to develop strategies to keep going. They must have a go at the spelling or find a way to indicate their meaning until they can get the help they want. There will always be children who are reluctant to have a go, but on the whole we found that such periods did encourage children to take risks, particularly with spelling.

Children not only need to see how people write; they need to see what people write. A good reading program is essential to a good writing program because it is primarily through reading that children learn to construct written text. There is no doubt that TV looms large as a source of inspiration for children's writing, but it does not offer the same scope for exploring language and text construction as does reading. Children's writing very often demonstrates this: most teachers have experienced those lengthy, convoluted, often incoherent recreations of TV stories which children often write. However, children who have had a rich diet of literature turn to literature to help them solve their writing problems.

The effect of a literature-based program was evident in our class, particularly as the children began to move from relating personal experiences to narrative forms of writing. Their writing reflected not only their grasp of story structure but also the language of story. None demonstrated more clearly the relationship between writing and reading than did Megan.

Megan

Megan is a talented writer from a highly literate family in which reading and writing are day-to-day activities. Megan borrowed and read books from the local library. Among them were several stories about unicorns, in which she developed an interest, and a book by Michael Berenstain called *The Sorcerer's Scrap Book* (Random House, 1981). The structure of this book is rather unusual in that it's composed of a number of vignettes which form a scrapbook of the Sorcerer's life. The structure and the story made a considerable impression on Megan and she used it as a basis for her story writing. During the course of her writing she reborrowed the books to read at home, but all her writing was completed at school. The reborrowing enabled her to check details, but she was a little reluctant to admit to this strategy in case it was the 'wrong thing' to do.

What follows is a proofed version of Megan's story. By 'proofed' we mean that spelling and some punctuation have been standardised to enable the reader to reconstruct Megan's meaning more easily. The structure, the grammar, the words are hers.

THE SORCERER'S SCRAP BOOK

I am a sorcerer. I talk to the stars. I've searched and searched and those swiftnesses I smelled and I've dug up lots of bones. I've been to school. My teacher was called Mr. Bucket. I learned a great deal from him before he threw me out. One day I asked the stars who was dying next. 'This is the Duke,' they replied. 'The Duke is next,' they cried. So the sorcerer ran and he ran fast. The Duke was most astounded by this news and said, 'You are going to poison me by my wine,' and that is where this story begins.

I started reading about unicorns because I needed one. It said only a fair maiden who plays a flute may get a unicorn and the wild men of the jungle jump off trees and ride them for sport. It had a beard like a goat, legs like a horse, a body like a horse too and a horn like a . . . . . . What on earth does it look like? It's a funny sight to see. Now it is the unicorn hunt. I started looking for my spells, then I found the one I wanted.

IT WORKED!!!!!!!

We started searching south, east, north and west till we came to a cave, a dragon's cave. I said, 'Do unicorns live here?'

'UNICORNS!' bellowed a loud voice. 'No. I'm just a dragon,' and he started telling a strange tale.

The Dragon's Tale

Why, just the other day, I was walking along minding my own business and a fine lady came along. 'Nice day,' I said.

'EEEEEEK! A dragon.'

'I beg my pardon,' I said.

'EEEEEEK! A dragon.' Then a knight in shining armour came, pulled out his sword and hit me on the head. When I woke up I had a big lump on my head.

Now was that fair?

'Excuse us but we're looking for a unicorn.'

'Never mind me. I'm just a dragon.'

Next we came to a smelly swamp. This time there was a vulture so we left.
Next we came to a desert. We saw a phoenix so we went on. Then we saw a
leaf fall and a shiver in the trees. It was a unicorn.

I set a spell but unfortunately something went wrong . . . . . . What was it?
Gold dust, of course!

How To Make Gold
To make gold of fear, because of the flames, it is wise to eat white bread thickly
spread with butter and margarine. After twelve days it turns red. This is called
Lion's Blood. After twenty-four hours it turns bright red. This is called Dragon's
Venom.

We were about to give up when we saw the Duke's daughter, Whilhelmina.
She sat down and played the flute. Then the fearsome unicorn came.

The Net Set Up
The net was set up. The unicorn charged into the net. It was put in the Duke's
menagerie. He said it would not be killed but I did not trust him. Would you?

That night they set watch over the unicorn. The Duke came out to find the
unicorn free. The Duke saw his daughter hiding in the Shadows. 'I know you
rascal. It was you.'

'But it's not true.'

Then someone shouted, 'I know. Horn fall off. Horn fall off.' And so it had.
Just as deer shed their horns every year, unicorns shed their horn every thousand
years.

And so the Duke had his horn. That night they had a celebration. Then an
arrow hit the Duke on the hand. That night the Duke felt sick . . . in fact he died
. . . not from wine but the arrow. Now I've grown old. I've forgotten much and
learned much. But one thing I will always remember is . . . . . . the stars never lie.

This story represents quite an achievement since Megan was only six years old. When
she was asked what she meant by 'I've searched and searched and those swiftnesses
I've smelled', she replied, 'Well, it's magic, isn't it?' We had to agree.

While the Megans of this world may be few, observing them can provide us with
valuable lessons about written language development. Megan did just that. She
provided important demonstrations about spelling development and editing, which
will be discussed in succeeding chapters; our concern here is with how much her
writing owes to her reading. Her vocabulary, her sentence structure (which is
extremely sophisticated) and the complex story structure capture the language and
technique of the books she has read. This is more than retelling, but even if it were
not, it would still be impressive. Many children go through a period of copying, but
it takes a little more sophistication to borrow structure and ideas. It shows clearly
that Megan is sensitive to the demonstrations that her reading provides.

Time

It is appropriate to note at this point that Megan was the child who took a term to
write her story—this story. So often teaching is judged by the quantity of its products,

not the quality. We were a little concerned that Megan was well into the term and had nothing that was finished. The concern, of course, was ours and not Megan's. However, we did not interfere. There are those with whom lack of product may be a problem, but Megan was clearly not one of them. Real growth occurred in her writing when she was not only given control over the writing process but control over time. This came about because the class decided to produce a magazine for themselves and their families. At the end of the term every child would submit one or two items for publication. For some this meant selecting one piece from many; for others, settling down and actually producing a piece for this purpose, and for Megan it meant that she had time to get to work on a story in her head.

Children like Megan are a challenge to teachers. They need time to develop their talents and we need to ensure that they get it. When it comes to writing, we need to emphasise quality, not quantity. The next year Megan went with her family to Canada, where she found that the learning environment at her school was very different. It prompted the letter shown opposite. Megan makes it perfectly clear what she considers writing is not. She also makes a subtle but powerful statement about time. She is doing so much busy work that she hasn't time to write as she did back in Australia.

Quality needs time to develop and this is as true of reading as it is of writing. It's not uncommon to see children being rewarded for the number of books read rather than the quality of that reading. You have only to walk into school libraries and classrooms and see lists of children's names and the books they have read to realise that quantity is a measure of success.

Strategies

What makes Megan a talented writer is primarily her ability to respond to reading as a writer and to use what she learns in her writing. Megan's success provides clues as to how we might go about helping other learners. To develop as writers children must read, but they must read with a writer's sensitivity. It would seem, therefore, that the best way we can help children to develop as writers is to ensure that they have a reading program which includes good children's literature and a variety of text types, and then to develop reading strategies which will draw their attention to those things that writers need to know. We also need strategies which will tackle specific problems that children may be having with text construction.

Schema Stories

One example of a strategy which sensitises learners to the way text is constructed is Carolyn Burke's Story Schema. This involves taking a well-known story, breaking it into chunks at transition points in the narrative, sharing these around among the children and having them reconstruct the story. It is important to discuss this process: 'Who has the next piece?' . . . 'How do you know you have the next piece?' . . . We found this strategy helped to improve story writing because it helped children understand coherence and structure. It can also be used with older children and with

22/5/1984

Dear Miss Bean✿

Last weekend we went to Olympic

Natoinal Park. I was sick...

But I am felling better now.

At scho✿l we arnt doing any writing

But we do diary, Phoｌnice questoins

Skillpack ｠cards then after Recese we

do∧spelling poem, spelling test Running writing

｠Arithmetice. Then after lunch we goｓ to

ｓｒlibrary then we do Art. They shure

keep us ▰ buｒsy. When we get finished

erly we do writing but the ▰▰ techer

chooses the topics and we have to

write it neatly with fullstops and

Capitals at the start ◊ of sent-eates◦

other types of text. However, when you are using non-narrative text, the learner should have all the pieces. Whereas narrative has a clear and relatively fixed structure that can be relied on to reconstruct the text, structure is less clearly defined in other types of text and depends more on their subject and purpose, so that you need all the pieces before you can decide how they fit together. Indeed there are often several acceptable ways of reassembling the same text, and discussing these helps to develop logical thinking. Although we have not worked as intensively with older children and non-narrative text, we have found that the strategy works well when you make a game of it. The idea is to get as close to the author's text as possible.

Any encounter with reading will provide demonstrations for the writer, but there are strategies which, though designed to assist comprehension, make these demonstrations more explicit. So, in addition to Story Schema, we have used several of Terry Johnson's literature strategies, in particular Literary Sociograms and Story Mapping. The first strategy involves listing the characters in a story and then working out the relationships between them. However, we found that the sociograms which our K-2 class produced were fairly simplistic because they lacked the language to describe relationships except in a fairly simplistic way. The second strategy involves mapping the world created by the story. We found that what the children did naturally was to map the sequence of the story and we encouraged this.

These and other similar strategies are fully described in Johnson & Louis (1985). Although the strategies are powerful in that they support both reading and writing, there is always the danger that overusing them will destroy children's love for literature. Literature is to be enjoyed, and nothing kills enjoyment so much as knowing that when the story is finished you will have to analyse it in some way. Such strategies need to be used selectively and sparingly, in our opinion.

Strategies for dealing with specific problems will naturally depend on the problem. The strategies that follow are certainly not exhaustive. They simply reflect some of the problems which we tried to deal with in our class, and because the children were at the time mainly concerned with story, they relate to narrative. However, some can be adapted for use with other kinds of text. It's also worth noting that these strategies are not new; they have been around, in some form or other, for a long time. There has been a tendency in process-writing classrooms to abandon many useful strategies. Although there is no doubt that many past practices are incompatible with the beliefs which underpin process writing, this is not true of all. There are teaching strategies which, with some adjustment, are consistent with such beliefs and so are appropriate for such classrooms.

Wordless Picture Books

These are helpful for young writers who find it difficult to sustain or sequence a story. The pictures provide a story-line which the writer can use to create a story. Because the pictures support writers with sequence and structure, it is easier to maintain sequence and structure during writing. There are numbers of commercially available wordless picture books, but a good alternative source is old reading schemes. Some early readers have excellent picture sequences but stilted, 'unnatural' text. Such text can be whited out to turn the readers into wordless picture books. For longer life white opaque tape or Contact can be used to obliterate text. If the child then uses water-based texta to write the story, the book can be reused by others.

Picture sequences can also be used for supporting writers in the creation of certain types of non-narrative text, particularly those which require temporal sequencing, e.g. describing a science experiment or a manufacturing process. Such sequences usually have to be devised by the teacher, but they can be devised by the writer as a prelude to writing.

Please Finish the Story

This strategy is exactly what its name implies. The writer is given the beginning of a story and is asked to complete it. Although we did not use it in our K-2 group, we have used it and seen it used quite successfully with older groups, and so we include it here. It helps those writers who struggle to maintain a story by relieving them of the necessity of getting started and freeing them to concentrate on the body of it. We find that many young writers can usually get a good start to a story but tend to collapse in the middle. The interesting thing is that older children, particularly if they are readers, seem to continue their story in the style of the original writer, which suggests that there may be some potential for using the strategy to focus on style.

Make Your Own Adventure

This is largely an extension of the previous strategy and borrows from the formula of the 'Make Your Own Adventure' series (Bantam). In these stories the reader is the central character. The chapters are very short and at the end of each the reader has to choose between two courses of action. Which page you read next depends upon your decision. As there are a number of decision points, there are quite a number of possible combinations and thus quite a number of different stories. Although not great literary works, these books are rather fun. We know of one adult who spent a sleepless night trying to discover the combinations which would get her through one story alive! The teacher can share the writing with a child or stories can be written as a class activity. One child writes what will happen if you do one thing, another what will happen if you make the other choice. Children enjoy writing such episodes and they are excellent for those young writers who seem to think that quantity is all. The strategy naturally constrains the amount of writing, so that it becomes manageable and amenable to conferencing.

Spelling

By encouraging learners to look at the structure of text and by developing strategies to tackle problems of text construction, we are certainly involving children in reading and writing, and consequently in spelling. However, at the risk of being repetitive, we again wish to emphasise that standard spelling is not the major issue at this point in the writing process, and it is extremely important that it does not become so. The greatest barrier to writing and spelling development is the excessive emphasis given to standard spelling before children even put pen to paper. This emphasis inhibits writing and so reduces opportunities to learn about spelling. What matters during initial composing is that children develop spelling strategies which enable them to write with a degree of fluency. Given opportunities to read and write such as we have described, they will learn to do this. Standard spelling is the consequence of writing and reading, not the access to it. This is not to say that standard spelling is unimportant, but rather that standard spelling is of little consequence if you do not write. Writing comes first!

STRATEGY LESSON PLANS

Story Schema

Rationale
Narrative has a clearly defined structure, composed of a number of transition points around which shifts in plot and theme are organised. To the reader, these transition points are major points for prediction. Getting readers to focus on transition points can help them develop an understanding of story structure that will assist them in their reading and writing.

Learner suitability
This strategy is useful for all readers and writers, as understanding text structure is crucial to both reading and writing.

Materials required
Familiar stories.

Procedure
Divide the story into a number of parts. The number will depend on the story and the level of the class. Divisions should be made at the major transition points in the story, and the reader should be able to predict what comes next. Share the story pieces amongst the group and get them to reconstruct the story. Ask 'Who has the beginning? . . . How do you know you have the beginning?' and so on. The children each justify their turns and read their pieces until the story is complete.

This strategy may be adapted to non-narrative text, but then readers must have all pieces of the text before them. Individuals or small groups can use this version.

Wordless Picture Books

Rationale
Pictures convey meaning. They are often used together with print to construct meaning, e.g. picture books. This system of meaning can be used to support young writers in constructing text.

Learner suitability
This strategy is suitable for all writers, especially those who need a supporting structure for writing stories, e.g. those who have difficulty sequencing events or those who are unable to maintain a coherent story-line.

Materials required
Picture books (wordless). There are commercially available books, or books can be made by using old readers or picture cut-outs. The pictures should 'tell' a clearly sequenced story.

Procedure
Show the picture book to the child and discuss the story. Have the child write the story making use of the pictures to maintain the story-line.

This strategy can be adapted to non-narrative text that involves temporal sequencing, e.g. describing how to construct something, a process, a science experiment, etc.

Please Finish the Story

Rationale
A narrative sequence consists of a temporal and spatial orientation, a complication or series of complications, and a resolution. By manipulating text we can force writers to focus on one or other of these aspects of narrative.

Learner suitability
This strategy is suitable for learners who find it difficult to maintain a story. Finishing the story forces them to focus on creating the middle and end rather than just the beginning.

Materials required
A collection of story beginnings. For example:

> A man called Mr Jones and his wife lived near the sea. One stormy night Mr Jones was in his garden when he saw the holly tree by his gate begin to toss and shake.
>
> A voice cried, 'Help me! I'm stuck in the tree! Help me, or the storm will go on all night.'
>
> Very surprised, Mr Jones walked down to the tree. In the middle of it was a tall man with a long grey cloak, and a long grey beard, and the brightest eyes you ever saw . . . .
>
> (Joan Aiken, *A Necklace of Raindrops*, Puffin, 1975)

> The Iron Man came to the top of the cliff.
>
> How far had he walked? Nobody knows. Where had he come from? Nobody knows. How was he made? Nobody knows.
>
> Taller than a house, the Iron Man stood at the top of the cliff, on the very brink, in the darkness . . . .
>
> (Ted Hughes, *The Iron Man*, Faber, 1968)

Procedure
Allow the children to select a beginning. Spend some minutes talking with each of them about their ideas for the continuation of the story before they write it. When they have completed their stories, they can be encouraged to read the stories from which the beginnings came.

Make Your Own Adventure

Rationale
We learn to write by being exposed to a variety of written texts and by having opportunities to write. Writers can be encouraged to write by modelling their writing on different kinds of text.

Learner suitability
This strategy is suitable for all learners but is particularly useful for those who tend to write long, convoluted stories. The model constrains them to brevity and a tight structure.

Materials required
A collection of 'Make Your Own Adventure' books (Bantam). These are inexpensive paperbacks, freely available at bookshops and larger newsagents.

Procedure
Encourage children to read several of these books, or read them with the children. You or one of the children can start the story, taking it up to the first complication, which must require a decision to do one of two things. The text is then given to two other writers, one of whom writes about the consequence of one decision, while the other writes about the second. Stories can be extended by a series of decision points, although they have more cohesion if these are restricted. The writing is cumulative, and not all writers can be involved at once. At the end collect texts and turn them into a class story.

Writing which results from these and other strategies we have discussed still requires audience and purpose, and, where these demand it, editing and proofreading. These strategies assist writing. They are not alternatives to a process approach to writing.

Chapter Six

EDITING

In many ways the distinctions between focusing, composing, editing and proofreading are convenient rather than real. Focusing assumes composing, and editing is in a sense recomposing. What we are dealing with are points along a progression. Editing is that recomposing which goes on after the initial text has been created and is very often self-initiated. The writer stands outside the text and views it as a reader. Even for the most efficient writers, however, there will be times when their closeness to the text makes them feel that they cannot distance themselves sufficiently as readers. At such times feedback from other readers is essential.

If at times feedback is essential for efficient writers, it is crucial for learners. Children need to know how successful they have been in constructing meaning: they need to 'test' their writing against the reactions of others. Such feedback is important during and after the process of writing. We have already mentioned the importance of a responsive audience for children's writing and so we will not belabour the point. Our main concern here is with feedback during the process, which raises the question of conferencing, since this is the principal means of providing such feedback.

Conferencing

Much has been written about conferencing and it is not our intention to cover ground already well covered by other writers, e.g. in PEN 53 (Roberts 1985). However, since conferencing is central to the whole process-writing approach, and to our approach, it is necessary to say something about it. Although the emphasis on teacher/pupil interaction can only be applauded, we have not been entirely comfortable with some aspects of current practice. It seemed to us that conferencing had become a methodology for teaching writing rather than an approach to the teaching/learning situation. We would argue that if it has value—and we believe it has—its use cannot be restricted to writing alone.

Moreover, because it had become a methodology, a natural classroom practice had become prescribed, with the result that many teachers had begun to feel awkward about it. We cannot conceive of any teacher worthy of the name who would not talk with children about some aspect of their learning during the course of the school day. What is this if it is not a conference? We found ourselves, like many other teachers, becoming more than a little anxious about something we had been doing for as long as we had been teaching.

This is not to diminish much of what has been said and written about conferencing. Apart from causing us to rethink our beliefs about writing, the real value of Graves' work is not that he introduced the writing conference, but that he forced us to look at the kinds of interactions we had with children when we taught writing. It was not a question of introducing something new, another teaching fad, but rather of improving what most of us were already doing in some way or another.

We began by trying to improve the interactions that already existed between the children and ourselves. These were certainly not confined to writing, but because our focus was largely on writing, the writing conference was our main concern. When we started neither of us felt we did it well, and in retrospect it was obvious that we did not. Despite our efforts to be otherwise, we found that we still had a tendency to be verbal red pens. It's easy to excuse this by saying old habits die hard, but we have come to believe that this explanation is far too simplistic. The truth of the matter is that we were often not in control of our conferencing, especially when the children were not in control of their writing. Because they were not in control, we did not know where to begin to help them; i.e. we were not in control either. In such a situation it is very easy to fall into the trap of reasserting your control by becoming a verbal red pen, and then it is generally the surface features of the language that become the focus of attention. We have done it and we have observed others doing it.

Not surprisingly, as we worked on the business of giving children control in the manner that we have described in previous chapters, our conferencing improved. We found that we spent less time with each child because the problems were not so overwhelming. Consequently we could see how to focus our conferences better, so that while we spent less time with individuals, the time was more profitably spent. There were children who took more of our time than others, but they were children who needed it. Dealing with large numbers also ceased to be the problem it had been.

Working on the issue of learner control also changed the kind of conferencing that was going on. At the start teacher conferencing predominated, though peer conferencing occurred quite naturally too and we encouraged it. There is no denying that the teacher/learner conference is important, but it seemed to us that learner control should also include control in the conference. We felt that children could exercise more control over identifying and dealing with some of their own problems, and so we decided to make greater use of group conferences to encourage self-reliance. These did not become substitutes for teacher/learner conferencing, but they did reduce the need for it. We ultimately found we achieved more through being members of a group than we were achieving in many of our individual conferences.

Our early group conferences were not a great success: we heard ourselves being echoed by the children and we cringed. This was when we began to fully realise the shortcomings of our conferencing. Apart from that, the interaction we had hoped for seemed to be missing, and it took us a little time to understand why. Children will play and talk together in groups without too much trouble, but what we were demanding was something more. We were asking them to *work together*, and to do this they needed to learn how to talk and listen effectively in groups. Most had no difficulty sharing their work—indeed they were more than eager—but their eagerness often made them less willing to listen and respond to others. What they lacked were the techniques of grouptalk. Our writing program had already extended into reading, and now we found ourselves facing an oral language problem. It led to a revamping of what is commonly known as Newstime—that time at the beginning of the day when children usually share items of news.

Grouptalk

We simplified Whipple's (1975) rules of grouptalk, wrote them out and displayed them in a prominent position.

UNDERSTAND

CONTRIBUTE

STICK TO THE SUBJECT

LISTEN

RESPOND

SUM UP AT THE END

These rules were discussed with the class so that the children had a clear understanding of what they meant. The children were divided into groups of five or six (six is considered an ideal number for group interaction). Groups remained static for a reasonable time to allow children to develop a sense of belonging (constant changes create unstable group dynamics which can be counter-productive). At the beginning of each week the class selected six topics for discussion during that week and these were listed on the board and numbered. As the children went to their groups each morning they were given a number corresponding to a topic. This number would change each day so that children got a different topic each day. Number one would be called upon to speak for one minute on that topic while the group members listened and then responded. Number two would speak on topic two and so on. At the end one person from each group would be called upon to speak to the class in order to give the children experience with a larger group. During these sessions one or both of us would monitor a group and then talk with the children about how well they were able to follow the 'rules'.

The next step was to move the children into longer and more focused discussion, so that they discussed one topic for the period. We found that these topics were best posed in the form of a simple question to which the group had to provide an answer. Questions might range from how to raise some money to who might be invited to talk about hobbies. (It was discussion about fund-raising that led to the production of the *Family Blue* magazine, a profitable venture as the magazine was much in demand.) At the end of the discussion one member of the group was called upon to sum up by presenting the decision of the group and the reasons for it. We found that as children's grouptalk improved, so did the group conferences, and what we discuss next is in essence a form of grouptalk.

Summing up after a grouptalk session.

Author's Circle

This was the name we gave to our group conferences which provided an opportunity for children to get feedback on their writing. At first they were comparatively formal. We specified the groups and the rules were quite clear. Nobody could come to the group without a piece of writing to share, ourselves included, and each one had to attend a group once a week. In retrospect this seems very restrictive and to some extent it was, but we found it better to err on the side of formality when we were feeling our own way. It's easier to let go than to try and tighten up when things go wrong.

Once these groups began to operate reasonably well, the children organised their own conferences when they needed them. They would simply announce that they required a conference and invite others who were also ready to join them. Our responsibility was to see that the groups did not get too big and to encourage one or two 'reluctant' participants when appropriate. We made it a practice that one or other of us would join Author's Circle. Indeed this is imperative at the start (though as parents became involved they took over this role). Children have to learn what kind of questions to ask: they need teacher demonstrations and learn very quickly from such models, as we had already discovered. Even when they were able to ask appropriate questions, we continued the practice of joining the circle to maintain our own membership of the writing community and to identify any problems arising.

Once the Author's Circle was gathered, the members took it in turns to share their piece or part of a piece, depending on whether they were seeking a reaction to the whole or help with a particular part. Other members of the group listened to the reading and then responded. We encouraged the children to respond by asking a question of the author rather than simply offering comment. We found comments tended to be trivial and of little real help to the writer, though there were times when they were entirely appropriate. After everybody in the group had reacted, we would summarise the reactions so that the writer received a clear message about the effect of the piece or the help required. The summary did not impose any obligation on the writer to respond; it was no more than a restatement of what had been said.

The teacher's role in an Author's Circle is a subtle one. The teacher is required to give example and direction without dominating, as in the following transcript from one of our Author's Circles (where the adult was Christine Walsh). Young Jane had finished her story and wished to share it.

THE RAINDROP THAT FELL

Once upon a time there was a raindrop. One day he was sitting on a cloud. He was dancing and dancing until he fell off the cloud and he fell into a river. Then the river took him very far away. It took him down to the sea and then a wind came up and took him out of the sea. It blew him onto the sand. He was walking on the sand and he saw a boy building a sand castle. It had a moat in it. It went into the sea. He walked to the sand castle. He was watching the boy when the storm came. Then a light bulb came down. He climbed up it and lived happily ever after. THE END.

ANDREW: What do you mean, a light bulb came down?

JANE: Well, it came down. It was like a staircase, so he walked up it and went back onto the cloud and he jumped onto the cloud.

RENAE: What was the raindrop's name?

JANE: I haven't given it a name. I can't think of one.

C.W: I want to know what your light bulb looked like. Was it like one of those (*pointing to the fluorescent light*) or was it the sort of thing that's shaped like a pear that you have at home? What did it look like?

JANE: It came down like a staircase.

C.W: And it was a light bulb?

JANE: Yes.

C.W: What's a light bulb? I don't think I understand.

JANE: Lightning and it comes down lots of times.

C.W: A lightning bolt! I thought it was a light bulb. It's a lightning bolt and it's a ziggy-zaggy thing. O lovely! I know. Great!

RENAE: What were his mum and dad's name?

JANE: He didn't have a mum and dad because they fell in the river.

These are first-graders, yet with a little help their circle becomes a real learning experience. Andrew immediately sees the major problem in the story and asks what Jane means. This is clearly the point that needs to be followed up, but Renae's concern with names is in danger of causing a digression. Without taking control away from the children, Christine steps in to help Andrew pursue his concern and to clarify meaning for Jane, showing her quite clearly where the confusion occurs. Renae is certainly not put off and once again returns to her preoccupation with names.

Giving feedback to young writers does not necessarily mean they will act upon it. For some young writers the act of producing a written message is effort enough, and once something is written they are unwilling to make any changes. Giving the children audiences for their writing and providing demonstrations through our own writing helped us to overcome some of this reluctance. Once children learn that crossing out, inserting, and cutting and pasting are acceptable in drafts, they are less reluctant to edit. For several of the children who lacked fine motor control the physical act of writing was a problem, and we sometimes helped them make their changes or allowed them to dictate directly to the mother who volunteered to do some typing for us. We also discovered that children who brought what they considered 'finished' pieces to Author's Circle were understandably less willing to edit, and so we added another rule:

A WRITER SHOULD NOT COME TO AUTHOR'S CIRCLE WITH A FINISHED PIECE.

Another forum can be established for sharing finished writing.

Over time the children showed greater willingness to edit as well as greater sophistication in their responses to each other, as the following discussion of Russell's inventions shows. Russell had created and drawn a number of inventions, which he had then described.

RUSSELL:	(*showing his drawings*) This car invention is a car that can pick up paper and it can climb a hill too . . . (*pause*). And that's the suction pump at the front and there's the hill (*pointing to drawing*).
	This motor bike can jump fire and a car too. There's the fire and car (*pointing to drawing*). The petrol tank is at the front not at the back.
W.B:	Why would that be?
RUSSELL:	Because if you have it there, right there, it gets too hot when he puts his feet down.
JANE:	Where did you get the idea of doing inventions?
RUSSELL:	I just saw these *Towards 2,000* on TV and thought I would make a story about a few inventions I made up.
JANE:	Are you going to make up any more inventions?
RUSSELL:	I might make up a story about it. I don't know yet.
W.B:	Show me your second-last invention. You've got a suction cap at the front going up the hill. Why do you need that?
RUSSELL:	Because it picks up paper.
W.B:	Where does the paper go?
RUSSELL:	It goes in under those big bits there, then you take the seat up and empty the bits of paper.
W.B:	It's a storage bit, is it?
JANE:	I thought it would be for the roads, so it could pick up bits and pieces off the roads.
RENAE:	I thought it could pick it up and throw it to the tip. It doesn't have to take it home.
W.B:	Do you think it takes it back so all the scrap paper can be used for something else? It's a recycling kind of a thing, is it?
RUSSELL:	Yes.
JANE:	Like making it into newspaper?
RUSSELL:	I will put some more bits in with arrows and put things in people asked me.

This snippet of Author's Circle shows a real growth in the children's confidence and the way they are able to discuss issues of meaning and clarification. Russell is able to assess the situation and terminates the discussion by saying what action he plans to take. The extent of this growth was demonstrated one day when we were accosted by several of the kindergarteners demanding to know why they could not join Author's Circle. At the time most of them were still not able to produce a clearly identifiable message and, considering this, we had not insisted that they join Author's Circle, although they had opportunities to share what they had done with us and their peers. Our reasons were certainly not substantial enough to refuse them, and so they brought their messages, composed of drawings and letters, to an Author's Circle. They then proceeded to discuss their messages and drawings with as much aplomb as any of the second-graders. After that they regularly joined the Circles.

Another incident not long after that with the kindergarteners showed us the potential of Author's Circle. One day we arrived at school after a social evening the previous night. (It's easy to talk about teaching as if nothing exists for teachers beyond

Author's Circle.

it.) Neither of us had any writing to share but we wanted to join an Author's Circle. So, instead of our own writing, we took a piece by a well-known children's author. We told the children that it was not our writing but we would like their reaction to it. They proceeded to discuss it with as much sophistication and confidence as they discussed Russell's inventions. Unfortunately in our disorganisation we did not have the tape-recorder handy. However, we afterwards made it a practice to slip a piece of writing by a renowned author into Author's Circle from time to time. It made the children feel part of a writing community and encouraged them to read with a writer's perception.

Author's Circles helped children to fill gaps and eliminate nonsense, i.e. to undertake basic editing, but if they were to develop and refine their ability to edit, they had to be extended beyond this. They had to understand that writing is about language choices, that subtle changes in language can alter meaning and the way it is perceived by the reader. To help them develop such understandings we made use of a number of strategies. However, as we pointed out at the beginning of the chapter, the distinction between editing and composing is more one of sequence than substance, and so these strategies are as much about composing as editing.

Think me a Poem

This strategy was originally developed by Bouffler to encourage the writing of free verse. However, it also demonstrates how language choices can affect meaning. It involves free association around a topic. Children are asked to supply words, sentences or phrases that come to mind when they think about the topic, and these are collected on the board or O.H. projector, or on pieces of paper. The idea is then to organise them in some way so as to create a sense of the subject which can be presented as a free-form poem. It's best to begin with a class demonstration in which everyone works with the same set of ideas. When you ask children where they wish to begin you seldom get consensus, and so for demonstration purposes you have to settle on one schema. However, when you have demonstrated the strategy, the children can be invited to go with their own choice. The same set of ideas yields many different meanings.

Young children will simply make lists in the beginning. It may take several demonstrations and a little support to get them to organise the ideas, but it is well worth the effort, especially when the class is able to give a choral presentation of its own poetry at a general assembly. With young children we present and type their poems, which means that we make decisions about punctuation and lay-out. Doing this in front of the writer provides an excellent opportunity for demonstration, and we found that it wasn't long before the children could attempt their own. It's not uncommon for questions of syntax to arise. Should the word be 'quick' or 'quickly'? Should we put an 'and' in there, or is it better left out? On one occasion an argument over where a particular line should go led to a discussion about refrains and several days of searching out and reading poems which had refrains. This is one of our more powerful strategies because it has the potential to be used in a number of ways—and with any writer from five to ninety-five! The following is the work of a group of second-graders, who turned the ideas listed in the left-hand column into the poem on the right.

	WINTER
Cold	Cold!
Foggy morning	Hard to get out of bed.
Damp	Woolly jumpers and gloves.
Frost	Damp, foggy morning
Hard to get out of bed	Frost!
Warm fires	Ice on the windscreen.
I run to school	Car won't start.
Warm	I run to school.
Smoky breath	Cold hands
Red nose	Red nose
Ice on the windscreen	Smoky breath.
Cold hands	Warm fires.
Car won't start	WARM.

Synonym Substitution

Although Crafton developed this as a reading strategy, we have extended it to focus children's attention on word choice. It is generally used with early readers and involves giving them a familiar story in which certain words have been underlined. They read the story together, substituting a word of similar meaning for each word underlined. We had used it as a reading strategy but only realised its potential for writing late in the year, so that we have not had a great many opportunities to work with it. While the children are making the substitutions we jot down as many as we can. Then we go back and look at them, discussing whether they are real alternatives or not. The focus on words and their meanings also provides opportunities to focus on spelling.

Logical Connections

Success at school demands that children be able to develop logical arguments and present them in writing. The conventions of cause and effect have to be understood. Children have to be able to use logical markers, such as 'because, therefore, consequently, moreover' and so on. While these conventions were not an issue in our K-2 class, they certainly become so as children move through primary school and on to high school. For this reason we are including here a strategy developed by Christine Walsh. We have found it very effective for teaching 'because' and 'therefore' and the reasoning signalled by these words.

The strategy is not unlike the Bundling and Think me a Poem strategies, except that the resulting text deals with cause-and-effect explanations. It is best done with an O.H. projector and transparency strips, but strips of paper can be used with a small group. After facts about the subject have been assembled on the strips, they are arranged in sequence to reveal any gaps in the logic. Christine provides the following example based on the transportation of convicts. The list of facts the students came up with was:

> First Fleet came to Botany Bay
> England wanted to get rid of convicts
> Convicts had to work like slaves
> Many people in England were very poor
> Prisons were overcrowded
> Long journey—many convicts died
> People jailed for quite small crimes
> Convicts sent to America
> England wanted a new place for convicts.

A tentative rearrangement of these facts revealed gaps in the logic: for example, why did England want a new place? With prompting the children added:

> America became independent.

Once the gaps have been filled you can show possible ways of presenting the argument using 'because' and 'therefore'. For example, using $\therefore$ for 'therefore':

> Prisons in England overcrowded
>
> $\therefore$
>
> Convicts sent to America
>
>   but
>
> America became independent
>
> $\therefore$
>
> England wanted a new place.

By altering the symbol from ∴ to ∵ (for 'because') the above can be rearranged:

> Convicts had been sent to America
>
> ∵
>
> Prisons were overcrowded
>
> but
>
> England wanted a new place
>
> ∵
>
> America had become independent.

Inverting the symbol ∴ made it easy for children to see its transformation. (It is made even easier if the single dot is in a contrasting colour.) Children can easily grasp the necessity to change the order of thought to maintain the logic. In Christine's classes it is normal practice to check the logic of informational writing in this way:

- No BECAUSES reveals unsubstantiated assertions.
- No THEREFORES indicates evidence not leading to conclusions or general statements.

The Big Cloze

This strategy was developed by Noel Peters to assist second-language learners in Papua New Guinea, but we found that it has potential with mother-tongue learners too. Like the previous strategy, it can be used to help children develop connections. It involves the deletion of large chunks of text which the children have to fill in, as in this example:

> Mr. Brown took his umbrella because . . . . He enjoyed walking and thought it would be good exercise to walk. He had had bad toothache for several days, so . . . . He reached the dentist in 20 minutes. Because . . . . he sat down to read a magazine.

The strategy is particularly useful in helping children construct informational text where facts must be substantiated and conclusions drawn. We have become acutely aware that much more work needs to be done to help children develop logical thinking. Writing provides a powerful vehicle for doing this, but such strategies are only just a beginning.

STRATEGY LESSON PLANS

Grouptalk

Rationale

We learn through language. To learn effectively through oral language we must be able to listen as well as talk. We must also be able to argue, to consider, and to synthesise and develop ideas. Small group discussions—grouptalk—provide a forum for learning the rules of discussion and argument, which are central to developing these abilities, as well as opportunities for developing the abilities themselves.

Learner suitability
Suitable for all language users. The task needs to be adapted to the age and level of the participants.

Materials required
Only those required by the demands of the specific task.

Procedure
Divide the class into groups of six. Once formed these groups should remain stable for several weeks. Establish the rules of grouptalk. *Understand. Contribute. Be relevant. Listen. Respond. Sum up.* Set a topic for discussion (which will vary with the age and level of the group). At the beginning it is best set in the form of a problem that requires some consensus solution, e.g. What would happen if . . . ? Who should we invite to talk to us? How can we raise the money for our outing? The teacher should monitor the groups to see if they are keeping to the rules and talk about this with the children when the discussion is complete. With older children a group leader can be appointed as monitor of the rules, which means keeping the group on task and ensuring everyone contributes and sums up.

Author's Circle

Rationale
Writing is a complex process. When it is undertaken for audiences other than self, it demands that the writer be able to stand back from his/her efforts and assess the effectiveness of the communication as an audience reader might. The ability to do this develops over time, but all writers can be helped to develop it by getting an immediate audience response to their writing. Not only is feedback helpful for the writer, but encouraging writers to assume the role of critical and supportive readers helps them develop their own awareness of audience and its relationship to language choices.

Learner suitability
Suitable for all writers. It is more effective with writers who have some understanding of Grouptalk techniques.

Materials required
Each member of the group should have a draft of a written text. This should *not* be a final draft.

Procedure
Groups should be no more than six, including the teacher. The writer reads his/her piece. (It is important that the focus of this activity be on meaning, not on surface features of language—hence the reading.) The other members of the group are required to respond in turn. At the start, it is more effective if this response is in the form of a question to the author. The author has the right to respond to the question as he/she wishes. For young writers it is also helpful if the teacher sums up the responses of the group.

Think me a Poem

Rationale

Writing involves constantly making choices between alternative surface features in order to create meaning. Too often, however, concern for form takes precedence over meaning. Free-form poetry frees writers from many surface-feature constraints and allows them to choose on the basis of meaning rather than form.

Children often think of poetry as a 'special' kind of writing that conforms to a metre and rhyme scheme, but such constraints are not necessarily what makes poetry. This strategy may also serve as an introduction to poetry writing.

Learner suitability

Suitable for all beginning writers. It demonstrates that the same body of ideas and language can be arranged in different ways to create different meanings.

Materials required

Cards/scrap paper, pen/pencil.

Procedure

This strategy can be used with individuals, small groups or the whole class. Select a topic with the help of the children. Play an association game with the topic, jotting down any words, phrases or sentences which come to mind when the topic is suggested. Each word, phrase, etc. should be written on a separate card or piece of paper. Using the floor, or a table or board, have the children group ideas in ways that are meaningful. If this is done as a class activity an O.H. projector is invaluable, as then the words and phrases can simply be written on a transparency and cut up. There will be variations in the way children wish to group ideas. Allow them to develop their own organisation and discuss differences. The ideas can be presented as a free-form poem. With older children using this as a poetry strategy there is scope to look at published free-form poetry and the way that poets present it. Younger children may require additional help in deciding what message they wish to convey, and the teacher will need to assume responsibility for its presentation as a poem.

Synonym Substitution

Rationale

When we read we predict meaning by making use of our knowledge of the world and the cue systems of language, i.e. the semantic, grammatical and sound/symbol systems. However, the correspondence between what is written and what is read is not necessarily exact. Readers may vary the text and still retain meaning, and the substitution of synonyms demonstrates this.

While readers do not necessarily read what is written, writers may deliberately choose particular words to ensure that their meaning is conveyed. By focusing on substitutions from a writer's standpoint it is possible to examine nuances of meaning. Focus on words and meaning provides opportunities for focusing on spelling.

Learner suitability

As a reading strategy it is appropriate for readers who rely heavily on the use of sound/symbol cues or who produce miscues that fail to maintain meaning. As a writing strategy it has general application.

Materials required
A familiar story in which a selection of words with readily available synonyms is underlined.

Procedure
Display the story on an O.H. projector or provide children with copies. The children read the story together, maintaining a reasonable and steady pace. When they get to an underlined word they have to substitute a word of similar meaning for the one underlined. Each reader may provide his/her own substitution. At the end of the reading discuss some of the more interesting substitutions. When using the strategy as a writing activity, note the substitutions offered and discuss them, focusing on the reasons why the writer chose the original word in preference to others. It is possible in some circumstances that substitutions may convey meaning more precisely than the original choice.

Logical Connections

Rationale
When constructing text writers make use of a number of linguistic devices which ensure cohesion. Cause-and-effect relations are signalled by the use of such words as 'because' and 'therefore'.

Learner suitability
Suitable for writers who need to develop an understanding of cause-and-effect relationships and how they are conveyed in writing.

Materials required
An O.H. projector.

Procedure
This strategy relates to written argumentation. Choose an appropriate topic (social science and science are likely sources). Record what facts are known about the topic on a transparency. Cut them up and assemble them in a possible sequence, which should reveal any gaps in the information. Elicit the missing information from the class or group. Introduce children to the symbol for 'because'—∵—and then rearrange the facts making use of this symbol: e.g. 'The water is cold ∵ it comes from melting snow.' Having established this pattern, introduce children to the symbol for 'therefore'—∴—by inverting the 'because' symbol. Demonstrate how this also inverts the statement: 'It comes from melting snow ∴ the water is cold.' Encourage children to provide reasons for assertions and to draw conclusions from evidence.

The Big Cloze

Rationale
Informational text requires the writer to substantiate assertions and to draw conclusions from evidence recorded. Cause-and-effect relationships are signalled

linguistically by the juxtaposition of facts and by such words as: because, therefore, so, consequently, etc.

Learner suitability
Useful for all learners who need to develop logical thought and the ability to express it in writing.

Materials required
Text containing cause-and-effect relationships. Either the cause or the effect is deleted to create a big cloze.

Procedure
Provide children with a copy of the text. Have them complete the cloze by providing the cause or effect, as is appropriate. This can be done individually or co-operatively. Discuss the 'answers' in terms of their logic.

Chapter Seven

PROOFREADING AND SPELLING

The major focus during editing has been on making meaning clear. We now arrive at that point in the writing process when attention is shifted to the surface features of language. (However, this does not mean that surface features are not related to meaning—quite clearly they are. Punctuation can make a big difference to the way something is read.) Concern for the surface features of language commonly has to do with what most people would call 'getting it right'. It involves checking grammar, punctuation and, above all, spelling in order to detect deviations from the standard. The act of focusing on these issues we have called proofreading.

Although it is during proofreading that standard spelling becomes an issue in writing, it is as much through reading as writing that we learn to become standard spellers. So at this point it is appropriate to dwell a little on the nature of reading and the demands of proofreading before we discuss the teaching of standard spelling in greater detail.

Reading

Our understanding of reading is that it is a process of constructing meaning from print (or writing). While most would accept this definition, there is much debate as to how it is done. We draw on work in psychology—especially the psychology of perception, linguistics and psycholinguistics—for our explanation, which is that reading involves the prediction and confirmation of meaning on the basis of a sampling of the print before us. We sample the print, predict meaning, confirm or correct our prediction by further sampling, and so on. To make these predictions we make use of the reading context, our knowledge of the world in general and of the text world in particular, and our knowledge of semantic networks, of grammar and of sound/symbol relationships. The more we know about these, the more predictable the text and the easier it is to read, because we need less visual information from the page.

Reading a fairy story to the class is not difficult for us. We know our children. We know about the world of children's fairy stories. We know our language and the language of fairy stories. We know the sound/symbol system of the language. The chances are that we have read the story many times before. The amount of information the eyes have to gather for us to be able to construct meaning is less than we require to read an introduction to nuclear physics—unless, of course, we already have a knowledge of nuclear physics.

This theory of reading explains, among other things, why we sometimes do not see words on the page. We simply do not focus on every word as we read. We do not know exactly what information the eyes transmit to the brain, but it has been shown that eye movements during reading are quite random over the page (Kohlers 1968). Our eyes do not move in a regular left/right pattern and down the page as one might expect. The fact that we do not read every word has important implications for proofreading. You might try the following passage for yourself.

THE BOAT IN THE BASEMENT

A woman was building a boat in her basement.
When it was finished she couldn't get the
the boot out of the basement because it was
too wide to go though the door. So she had to
take the boat a part to get it out. Perhaps he
should of planned ahead.

(Gollasch 1980)

How many 'corrections' did you make? When we present this exercise to groups of teachers the count varies between three and six (in fact six are required). We must assume that all teachers are reasonably efficient readers, yet they vary in their ability to proofread. The reason is that they are efficient readers, and even when they know they are looking for deviations, they still read for meaning. When reading for meaning we do not read every word and so we are likely to miss some deviations, even in a passage of only a few lines. This holds true despite our efficiency as writers/spellers.

Standard spelling

Our beliefs about reading, together with those about language, writing and spelling which we have already outlined, have important consequences for teaching spelling. They suggest that:

1. Standard spelling should be taught through strategies which focus children's attention on words in context, i.e. words within the context of written text.
2. Children need to be taught to proofread, since effective reading strategies are not necessarily effective proofreading strategies.
3. Proofreading is likely to be more effective if a period of time is allowed to elapse between writing and proofreading.

Focusing on words

We have already suggested a number of strategies which focus children's attention on text and on words in text. Synonym Substitution, for example, forces the learner to focus on the meaning of words, a focus that can also assist standard spelling. However, the focus on spelling can be made more direct if teachers are attuned to the spelling demonstrations that written text provides and can highlight them.

One of our favourite books for language 'study' is Roald Dahl's *The BFG* (Puffin, 1984), which we read as a class story. Not everyone is a Roald Dahl fan, or so it seems from comments made to us by some teachers and librarians. We definitely are, and so were the children in the class. For those who are not familiar with it, *The BFG* is a delightful story about a self-taught giant who kidnaps the orphan Sophie because she sees him one night blowing dreams into the windows of boys and girls. Because he is self-taught, the giant's language is idiosyncratic and he has a tendency to create words. At one point in the story he is describing the various kinds of giants and tells Sophie, 'Giants is all cannibully and murderful.' After we finished the day's reading we got to wondering whether you could say 'murderful', and quite an animated discussion followed. At the end of it we had a list of similar words: beautiful, hopeful, wonderful, careful. We had discussed their meaning and their spelling and decided that these words were not the same as 'teaspoonful'; that you could not say 'weedful' even if the garden was full of weeds, and that murderful was fine because you could be full of murder.

All written text provides demonstrations of standard spelling, but texts like *The BFG* encapsulate these demonstrations in a way that highlights them. Christine Walsh introduced us to the poetry of Shel Silverstein and its potential for such demonstration. It is more suited to primary-age children. An example is 'The Turnable Twistable Man', which is full of '-able' compounds, providing an opportunity to highlight such words. Christine does this by remarking to the class that it is a good collection of words and writes a selection on the board, into which she slips 'possable'. It is not long before someone spots it. She then starts to change all the endings, which of course the children will not allow. They usually have little difficulty in working out the difference. 'Possible' does not mean able to be 'possed'. In this short demonstration the children have focused on meaning, on the morphemic structure of these words and on their spelling.

It is not fashionable these days to teach children anything about the history of their language: there is just too much else to be taught. We think this is something of a pity. Apart from the fact that it is as viable a form of study as any other, knowing a little about word derivations (etymology) has never been a handicap for us and often assists us with spelling. So often the clue to spelling a word is knowing what it means and how it acquired that meaning. A tertiary student recently illustrated this. Throughout an assignment she had misspelled the word 'tertiary', in reference to tertiary education. When asked what the word meant, she replied that it meant university or college education. But while it applies to that, it certainly doesn't mean that. It was pointed out to her that it comes from the Latin 'tertius', meaning 'third', and refers to the third level of education. Apparently from then on she had no trouble spelling it. We would hate to see children being subjected to exercises in Latin and Greek roots, but some incidental study of them can be a great help to spelling.

Dictation

Dictation can also be used to focus children's attention on words. However, it has to be dictation with a purpose. There is really no point in taking down dictation unless it is to record meaning. Dictation to test spelling is even less efficient than using a word list, and since test lists tell you no more than that a child can spell certain words in isolation, both are fairly pointless exercises. By its very nature dictation demands that the person taking it focus on meaning, but when the emphasis is on meaning the writer is less likely to be concerned with spelling. Consider what happens to your spelling when you are taking notes. To concentrate on meaning and spelling at the same time is a difficult task for a young writer. While it is true that a writer can proofread after taking dictation, children need a reason for both the dictation and the proofreading. Apart from testing spelling, we can see no point to most school dictations.

Dictation can be made meaningful, however, if the children have a reason for it. Walsh gives them a reason. She shares a joke, a limerick, a tongue-twister, a short poem—something they might like to take home and share with Mum, Dad or siblings. Once they agree that the item is worth sharing, she dictates it. The emphasis is on getting down the meaning. The children then need a reason to proofread what they have written and so she suggests that they might like to make a joke book—not just a book of jottings but a finished production. The children standardise their spelling and punctuation as a group, which provides opportunities to discuss spelling. They then transcribe their piece into the book. The transcription can be approached as a handwriting activity, providing a much more meaningful handwriting lesson as well.

Proofreading

We believe that children need to be taught to proofread. Although they learn readily enough the importance of standard spelling, their natural inclination is to read for meaning, which we have argued is not necessarily the most effective way to proofread. There are numbers of suggestions as to how proofreading is best done. Some say reading backwards enables you to look at just the words, but we find it very laborious, particularly for children. We favour the ruler method, which involves placing a ruler over the text and revealing it line by line. This enables you to focus on a line at a time.

Once again, it was the BFG who provided the children with an introduction to proofreading. The giant catches dreams and places them in bottles, which he labels in his own idiosyncratic syntax and spelling. He obviously needs help to label his bottles and we simply invited the children to help him. Once children identify the non-standard form, they can provide the standard form if they know it; otherwise they are encouraged to try several spellings and mark the one they think is most likely to be the standard. We don't allow fence-sitting, although there are no penalties for being wrong.

This, we hope, forces children to pay greater attention to the standard form of words and helps avoid the common problem of knowing the possible spellings of a word but not knowing which is the standard. In fact this is the greatest problem with

How do you spell 'forest'?

standard spelling. As eleven-year-old Gilda put it, 'Spelling is easy. It's getting it right that's the hard part.'

We were not involved in teaching dictionary skills to our class, though there is no doubt that they have to be taught in due course. In the beginning, however, it is wise to encourage children to rely on the print environment to find solutions to their standard spelling problems, which attunes them to looking more closely at print in the environment.

Although most writers will proofread immediately they have written something, it is best to allow the text to lie for a period before raising issues of spelling. The further away the writer is from the writing, the less predictable is the text when it is read. As we have argued, this gives the writer a greater chance of 'seeing' non-standard spelling. It is partly for this reason also that we prefer to use passages not written by our children for any class or group proofreading. Using a child's writing would scarcely be inconsistent with our theory, since it would be new to the rest of the class, but we think that there are inherent dangers to children's self-concepts. We have been told of an incident where a mother considered that using her son's writing for a group proofreading amounted to victimisation. A great deal depends upon the kind of co-operative learning attitude you are able to develop in your class. We certainly would not have anticipated any such problems, but it was not worth the risk. This issue also highlights the importance of getting parents on side, so that they have at least a rudimentary understanding of what is happening in their child's classroom.

Lists, rules and classroom changes

So far we have avoided commenting directly on some of the current practices used in the teaching of spelling. However, we would be shirking the issue if we failed to do so because of controversy. Other writers discussing spelling in relation to process writing have recommended the use of personal spelling lists and methods like 'Look, cover, write, check'. If by chance any of our children had decided of their own accord to keep a personal spelling list or to use the 'Look, cover, write, check' approach, we would not have discouraged them as we believe these approaches are preferable to memorising traditional lists. On the other hand we did not promote personal lists or the 'Look, cover, write, check' method. The latter, we believe, is but a sophisticated form of memorisation, and language is not learned by memorisation. The value of personal lists depends largely on how they are used: if they are merely a substitute for the more traditional lists, then we would have to reject them on theoretical grounds. However, in many cases they are used as a kind of personal dictionary, and while we have no theoretical objections to such use, we have no evidence of how effective it is. The difficulty with taking such a stance against current practices is that many people then assume that you are not teaching spelling. If you believe that spelling is a separate entity, then the assumption is true. If, on the other hand, you see spelling as an aspect of written language, then we hope we have established how spelling is an inseparable part of our written language program.

Any action research such as ours requires some kind of safeguard. Ours was that at the end of the year our children would be tested against other grades still using the Quota program. Both groups were given a set of words from the Dolch word list, and the results showed no significant difference between the two. We certainly could not claim that our children were better spellers but, conversely, it was evident that spelling lists did not make any significant difference. Similar tests were carried out in a Victorian school and equivalent results were obtained. The Victorian experience showed, however, that the children who had not used lists in their writing program attempted significantly more of the test words. In short, they were greater risk takers. We have not, as yet, a set of criteria that will measure the quality of writing, but probably, if such a measure existed, it would show significant differences between the two groups. There is no doubt in our minds that the difference would favour the non-list group.

For the same reason that we reject spelling lists, we also reject spelling schemes which aim to teach spelling by teaching spelling rules. Any speaker of English knows the rules of spoken English but this knowledge is largely intuitive. Knowing the rules is a consequence of learning the language, not an access to it. Although children are strongly influenced by the language that surrounds them, they learn it by first developing their own rules, which they refine as they gain more language experience. Learning to spell is part of learning language, and children learn to spell in the same way as they learn other aspects of language. We are not saying that children should never be taught any rules: in some circumstances it may be appropriate to draw attention to a rule. What we are talking about here is a deliberate and systematic teaching of rules. Quite apart from the fact that it is an 'unnatural' approach to language learning, there are just too many rules and too many exceptions. Given the limitations of memory, it is simply not an efficient approach.

We have argued that the alternative to lists and rules is an integrated reading and writing program. This is where change must begin. The recent focus on writing has brought about many positive changes in the teaching of writing, but you cannot have reading and writing programs which are diametrically opposed and not expect problems with spelling. Phonic and skill-based reading programs do not sit well with the principles of process writing. Not only do their views of language differ, their views of learning are also very different. Since the integration of reading and writing is so crucial to the development of standard spelling, such conflicts create problems for learners which may well affect their spelling development.

Spelling is part of writing

Many teachers who have already developed consistent reading and writing programs still see the abandonment of spelling lists in terms of abandoning the teaching of spelling. At the root of this attitude is the belief that spelling must be treated separately—a belief that almost defies rational argument. The treatment of spelling as separate from writing is so engrained in us through all our school experiences, both as pupils and teachers, that it has become a conceptual trap for a great many. Even though we accept arguments against the separation of spelling and writing at an intellectual level, old attitudes so colour our thinking that we often make the separation without being aware of it. The constant demand for in-service courses on spelling is testament to this. Teachers with well-established reading and writing programs, and with an excellent grasp of language principles and the principles of learning, still want to discuss spelling as a separate issue. Accepting the integrated nature of spelling at an intellectual level is a start, but if it does not change our way of viewing language and language learners, it is no more than an intellectual position. When we have accepted that spelling is not something separate from writing and reading, we have to stop talking and acting as though it were. Someone once likened change to an onion from which you peel off different layers. Once we accept the intellectual argument, it must become a commitment, and finally a way of teaching life.

We have put our case against traditional practices in teaching spelling strongly. It should not be assumed, however, that we are advocating the wholesale abandonment of these practices in schools. We believe, equally strongly, that change should be evolutionary, not revolutionary. Teaching is a learning process. We have to begin where we are, at our own state of evolution, and work from there. Although we are convinced that spelling lists have limited use in the learning of standard spelling, and that there is more to be gained from developing appropriate reading and writing programs, we did not arrive at this point overnight. It took us time, a lot of professional reading and much conferencing with children, with teachers and between ourselves. We went through a period of evolution that involved using personal lists, and we did not let go of them until the children in the class clearly demonstrated to us that they were unnecessary.

Given the very political nature of spelling, we would suggest that there are three criteria which need to be met before spelling lists are abandoned.

1. A teacher understands how language, including spelling, is learned.
2. A teacher has developed a theoretically consistent and integrated reading and writing program.
3. As far as possible, parents are informed and/or involved in the change.

We hope that we have already gone some way to helping teachers meet the first two of these criteria. We recognise that some fairly fundamental changes also have to take place in public thinking, and if at times we are tempted to think such changes are impossible, we simply remind ourselves of the tremendous changes that have already taken place in our attitude to writing.

Punctuation

Although it may seem something of an addendum, we cannot leave a discussion of the proofreading aspects of writing without making some comment about punctuation. Punctuation is as much a question of editing as of proofreading, but since it is something we always check at the end, we have included it here. In retrospect, this is not an area that has received a great deal of our attention—not because it is unimportant, but because we were too preoccupied with other issues.

The particular aspects of punctuation that we covered in our K-2 class were the full stop, question mark and direct speech. On the whole we dealt with questions of punctuation on an individual basis, with the emphasis on making sense. We have yet to find a better way of teaching full stops than the tried and true strategy of reading children's writing back to them exactly as they have written it.

Dealing with direct speech was always a little more difficult until we used a group strategy developed by Walsh. It involves using a text which includes a conversation between two speakers (the school magazine is a good source). All punctuation is removed. The children are then asked to identify the number of speakers and to underline what they say. In subsequent discussion they are led to see inverted commas as a kind of stylised speech bubble. The advantage of this is that you never see a speech bubble with punctuation outside it. All other speech punctuation, therefore, goes inside the inverted commas. For example:

how could you lose such a big school bag dannys mother said in a loud voice

dunno said danny i was sort of swinging it around by the handles coming home

over the foot bridge it sort of flew out of my hands and fell down onto a truck

on the freeway and of course you forgot to write your name and phone number

in it as i told you to said mrs hillery

(Robin Klein, *Hey Danny*)

Other types of punctuation can also be dealt with by using this or similar texts with punctuation removed.

STRATEGY LESSON PLANS

Help Me

Rationale
Proofreading asks writers to adopt the stance of a reader and to recognise non-standard spelling. Although the writer acts as a reader, proofreading differs from reading in that it requires the reader/writer to focus on each word in context. But because writers are very familiar with their own texts, they are highly predictable, and the more predictable a text is, the more likely it is that deviations will be overlooked. Thus it is easier to proofread another's writing.

Learner suitability
Suitable for all learners.

Materials required
A transparency of text in which there are non-standard spellings. An O.H. projector.

Procedure
Explain to the children that the writer needs help because others are going to read the text. Allow them to read it and select words they think are non-standard. When they think they have all the words, cover the text and reveal it line by line, asking them to check. Have them standardise the spelling. If they are unsure of the standard form, have them try as many ways as possible to spell the word. From these they must select the one they think is standard. Then give them the standard form and ask them to write it and compare it with their own versions.

   This activity may be done with a class but it is more effective with small groups. During its course children can be directed to appropriate spelling strategies, and meaning and morphemic units can be discussed.

That's Interesting

Rationale
Written text provides demonstrations of standard spelling. It is by reading with a writer's perception that we learn standard spelling.

Learner suitability
Suitable for all learners.

Materials required
Any written text, especially texts that by their nature draw attention to particular words. For example, Roald Dahl's BFG creates his own words; poetry often repeats words or 'plays' with them, e.g. 'The Turnable Twistable Man' in Shel Silverstein's *Light in the Attic* (Cape, 1982).

Procedure
Become aware of the demonstrations of standard spelling that text provides. When you have finished reading a text, draw children's attention to these demonstrations.

Focus on meaning as well as spelling. However, we read for meaning and enjoyment and so reading should not be interrupted to demonstrate a point. The strategy should be used appropriately and not become just another exercise.

Have You Heard This One?

Rationale
Writing is a process of recording meaning so that it may be reconstructed by a reader. Meaning is the basis for all writing. When writing is directed to an audience other than self, it is important that surface features be standardised.

Learner suitability
Suitable for all learners.

Materials required
A joke, riddle, tongue-twister or limerick that is likely to appeal to children. A small exercise book for each child.

Procedure
Share the joke, riddle or whatever with the children. Suggest that they might like to share it with others and dictate it to them. Tell them that you have other jokes and that perhaps they might like to keep a book of jokes and riddles. This is to be a handwritten publication. When they have taken down the joke or riddle they can transfer it to their book. Stress the importance of having standard spelling, grammar, etc, because this will be a finished publication. Children may need help in standardising their spelling, and so there is an opportunity for discussing spelling issues with them. The strategy also provides a focus for handwriting.

Who Said?

Rationale
Punctuation conventions are important because they assist readers to construct the meaning intended by the author. Text without punctuation is difficult to process.

Learner suitability
Suitable for all learners, especially those who are having difficulty with the punctuation of direct speech.

Materials required
A text which includes a conversation between two speakers and from which all punctuation has been removed. The strategy works best using an O.H. projector.

Procedure
Have the children read the text and then discuss difficulties they had with reading it. Ask them to underline what was said by the two speakers, using a different colour for each, and point out how messy this looks. Draw their attention to the way speech is shown in comic strips and ask them to draw speech bubbles around each speaker's words. This is messier still. The alternative then is to use a stylised speech bubble—inverted commas (*not* sixty-sixes and ninety-nines). Point out that nothing

goes outside a speech bubble in a comic, and that likewise all other speech punctuation goes inside the inverted commas.

Warning!

None of the strategies we have outlined in this book is intended to be the definitive answer to a particular language problem. We can only keep emphasising the fact that these are some of the strategies we have used to solve our problems. We have a particular theoretical orientation to language and have endeavoured to ensure that our strategies are consistent within that theoretical framework. All the strategies have been successful with some children, but there have been circumstances in which they did not achieve the desired result, and it was then necessary to develop different ones. If a strategy does not work it does not necessarily mean that it is useless, but rather that it is not appropriate to that situation.

Chapter Eight

ASSESSMENT AND REPORTING

One of the highlights of any country calendar is the local Show, including the various competitions usually associated with such events. The juvenile section of the Wagga Wagga Show includes a story-writing competition. Megan decided she would enter 'The Sorcerer's Scrapbook'. Although we knew she would be competing with children twice her age, we encouraged her. Megan did not even rate a mention, but it was not this that upset her. It was the fact that the judges did not believe she had written the story. As if to prove its authenticity, as much to herself as to the judges, Megan retrieved the story and worked on it some more.

Megan's experience raises some interesting questions about the assessment of writing. One can only speculate about the criteria the judges used in making their judgements, but clearly they had certain expectations about children's writing and about originality, and they were judging only Megan's product. Ultimately it is the product by which all writers are judged. Although, from a teaching point of view, judgements about the process may be of greater importance in assisting young writers to learn, it is the product about which parents, examiners and employers make judgements. The question, however, is: what are the criteria on which they base their judgements and how appropriate are they? The answer to that question requires a great deal of research, but if our own experiences are anything to go by, such criteria must be questioned. After Megan's experience we certainly began to question our own criteria and analyse our own judgements.

This introspection is far from complete, but we have managed to identify some of the factors affecting our judgements.

Judging products

We have argued that all language is context specific, and so it's necessary to make judgements about writing in the light of what we know of the context, particularly the topic, audience, purpose and text type. In broad terms there is nothing very startling about such a statement. We would not expect an essay written under exam conditions, without reference to any information other than what is in the writer's head, to be judged by the same criteria as one might use to judge a story written in the writer's own time. In reality, however, many of the criteria we use often become blurred or are used inappropriately. It is not uncommon to find readers judging very different kinds of text by very similar criteria, as we have found when we have asked teachers to make judgements about children's writing. Their judgements are, of course, greatly influenced by surface features. This is not surprising, however, since things like spelling, grammar, etc. are much easier to make judgements about and to quantify. Other criteria tend to be more nebulous and in general less well understood.

The difficulty of developing criteria for judging writing lies in the fact that every context is different. We have endeavoured to identify a set of general criteria on which to base our judgements because we must make judgements. We have to assess children to develop programs for them and we have to report on progress to parents. We still have some way to go before we can suggest with any confidence what these criteria for judgement may be. What follows looks at some of the questions we ask about writing and some of the limitations of these questions.

Topic

Does the writer have sufficient information about the topic? The importance of this question varies in relation to the purpose and type of writing the writer is engaged in. Although it is crucial to informational text, it also applies in story writing. Oversimplified stories are often the result of a lack of information, as young writers will tell you. 'I thought I could write a story about this, but when I came to do it I didn't have enough to write about.'

Are the ideas clearly presented? This question begs the issue somewhat. What do we mean by clearly presented? To us it means, first and foremost, asking whether there is a clearly discernible story-line, argument, sequence of events—an overall logic to the piece. Again, the nature of the logic in question depends upon the nature of the text. Is this 'logic' fully developed? Once again this depends on the nature of the text, but the question covers such things as unsubstantiated generalisations in the case of argument, or poorly developed story-line sequence in the case of story.

The story opposite provides an example of poor story logic. It's not uncommon to find this, especially when children start retelling TV programs. It seems to us that they tend to get caught up in the visual images rather than the story-line. The story is by a fifth-grader (we selected an older writer in this case because the problem is more clearly illustrated). Reading the story we can supply a probable sequence of events, but, as it stands, there is no logical connection between joining the army, throwing the grenade, saving lives and fighting the Germans.

Is the organisation of ideas appropriate? This is very much part of the previous question but relates to appropriateness rather than clarity. Are the ideas arranged in the most effective order? Is there too much emphasis on less important ideas, or not enough on crucial ones? Is all the material relevant? With younger writers the problem is often the omission of relevant material, which leads to a lack of

I N THE ARMY

17-6-86

It all started when I was walki-ng down the street a ARMY Seargeant grabbed me he said you look tough do you want to go in the ARMY I said WOW yes he said do you want to of course I do come with me young man you will look like this I said could I try a grenade yes BOOM Germans went sky high holey macrael the seargeant said you saved our lifes you should git a medal of honour BANG german tanks were coming quick run for cover I ran and jumped in a pit were a machine gun was then I started to shoot I shot a man on top with a machine gun I got a bazooka and blew one up the other ones turned away and went back then a

coherence—what we have loosely termed 'logic'. With older writers the problem becomes reversed and you get what is called padding, the inclusion of irrelevant material to make up the required length.

Are the ideas original or are they borrowed? This question is one that is generally asked about content, although the issue is not clear-cut for us. Clearly plagiarism is unacceptable, but many practices in schools tend to foster it. School projects and the ways children are encouraged to collect and use information often lead to plagiarism. However, when you move from the direct lifting of material to the 'borrowing' of ideas, the judgement becomes harder to make. This is particularly the case with young writers who retell or borrow from stories they have read to develop their own story. Megan provides a good example. Every story begets another story. We borrow ideas and structure, and so no story is entirely original. On the other hand, since each story is a product of the writer's own unique experience, every story is original in some way. Megan borrowed ideas and structure but gave them her own unique stamp, so that her story was in no way a retelling. At six, however, the magnitude of the task she undertook probably led her to borrow more than the judges felt was allowable. The difficulty lies in where you draw the line, especially with young writers.

We would argue that this retelling and borrowing behaviour is a plus rather than a minus for young writers. It provides them with opportunities for exploring and experimenting with story and book language. This is also true of older writers. Clearly we do not expect originality of ideas in most high-school writing tasks. What we are looking for is a synthesis of ideas expressed in the language of the writer. At the same time we expect writers to control the language of their subject, i.e. we expect them to write like text books. It is not surprising that many of them lift directly from their text books and continue to do so even after they enter tertiary education, although by then they understand the taboos against plagiarism and attempt to make changes in the text by using synonyms.

If originality is a criterion for judging writing—and we believe that to some degree it should be—then we have to be very clear about the kinds of originality we are looking for and provide more help for learners to achieve it. Some of the strategies we have already suggested will assist learners in making information their own.

Audience

We found that in our K-2 class questions about audience were a lot more difficult to ask. There is no doubt that the children had a sense of audience. They clearly knew who they were writing to, but it was more difficult to see how this sense of audience was reflected in what they wrote. The most obvious factor was their concern for the correctness of surface features. They understood the importance of correct spelling and grammar when their writing became public, e.g. when they wrote to the Queen. Apart from this, questions of inappropriate language, subject or style never arose. Here are some questions you may well ask, however.

> Is the language appropriate to the audience? Is it too esoteric? (But this is more often a problem with text books than children's writing!) Is it too colloquial?

> Is the style trite or bland? (We would usually label it boring.)

> Is the subject matter appropriate for the intended audience?

Purpose

This was not the issue with a K-2 class that it is likely to be with older and more sophisticated writers. Our main concern was to ensure that children had reasons to write. Such reasons usually determined the kind of text they wrote and to some extent the way they wrote. Our judgements were of a fairly gross kind: e.g. if the purpose was to produce something for inclusion in the *Family Blue* magazine, was the piece submitted suitable for inclusion? Purpose is clearly related to topic, audience and type of text, and in more sophisticated texts it is reflected in the subtle interplay of many of the factors already mentioned: choice of language, organisation, style, etc.

There is one general question that we ask regularly of writers: 'Why did you write this?' It might well be asked of the fifth-grader who produced 'In the Army'. What was his purpose? Was he telling a story, persuading us to join the army, giving us an idea of army life, or relating an incident in the war? Judging on the basis of the product alone it looks like none of these things, but simply writing for writing's sake. From a learning point of view we need to know more about the writer and what he thought he was doing than the writing itself reveals.

Type of text

Has the writer succeeded in producing the kind of text the situation demanded or that he/she set out to write? If the writing is a story, does it have the elements of story; if a report, is it written as a report, and so on? The important thing here is to consider the difficulty of the particular writing task. If we take Megan's story as an example, we can see that she has attempted a very difficult story structure, and possibly she will appear less successful than if she had played safe and followed a more traditional structure. Many of the critics of process writing often fall into the trap of comparing attempts at more sophisticated and difficult writing with the safe, often unimaginative, correctly spelled pieces that children wrote in the past. We all have to be more attuned to the demands of different kinds of text and take these into account when making judgements about children as writers. It is not enough, however, for teachers to do this; parents too need to be made aware of the kinds of criteria we are using.

Surface features

Do deviations in spelling, grammar and punctuation detract from the writing? This is an easy enough judgement to make. The problem is how much weight should be given to these things when we make our judgements. The answer lies partially in the audience and purpose for which the writing was intended and the writer's point of development. The experimentation of early writers must surely be judged differently from the deviations of sophisticated writers. The former may be judged in terms of spelling development. The latter may indicate a failure to proofread or a spelling problem.

Ultimately all judgements made about written texts are subjective. It is impossible to say what weighting should be given to the answers to any of the above questions, and herein lies the problem of assessing written language. The best we can really hope for is to ensure that our judgements are as informed as is possible. The factors that contribute to good writing are not well understood and attempting to identify our own criteria is only a start to understanding. We must emphasise that the list of questions we have suggested is in no way exhaustive. They result only from our introspection of our own judgements of children's writing.

Judging process

Judgements about products allow us to identify where the writer has succeeded or failed, but they do not provide teachers with the information necessary to assist the learner. And unless assessment provides us with such information, there is little point in it beyond establishing what children can or cannot do in a given situation. To assist writers we need to be able to make judgements about the way they write as well as what they write. The strategies in this book have to be developed around helping children in the process of writing, and this requires judgements about the process.

We began by asking ourselves what it is that good writers are able to do. Our starting point looked something like this.

Focus. Can select topics. Can collect and organise information for writing.

Compose. Can produce spellings that serve the purpose of recording meaning. Has a sense of audience and purpose. Can create a variety of written messages, each of which has its own features that are understood and used by the writer. (As appropriate, this would involve such things as developing a story-line or an argument, sequencing events and organising sentences and paragraphs. One could take each type of writing and develop specific criteria.)

Edit. Is willing to edit where appropriate. Can assume the role of a reader and identify points where meaning breaks down. Can make choices between language options and refine meaning.

Proofread. Can identify non-standard spelling or grammar. Can standardise it. Can use appropriate punctuation.

By making judgements about how writers are performing in relation to what may be considered appropriate writing behaviour, we can pinpoint where breakdowns are occurring in the process and offer support to the learner at these points. We hope that the strategies we have shared with you demonstrate how this may be done.

It is worth returning to Megan's story to see the importance of looking at process as well as product. The beginnings of her first and second drafts are shown opposite, the earlier one being on the left. When she dictated her story to the typist she made further changes, and so what we have is three different products at three different points in the writing process. It is impossible to show how Megan collected her information or how she returned to her sources during the writing, but the drafts provide an insight into her writing development which could not be revealed by one alone. Megan exhibits all the behaviour of an efficient writer. If we focus on her spelling, for example, we can see that there are changes from first to second draft. There is considerable evidence that Megan can recognise non-standard forms and in many cases standardise them. Teachers to whom we have shown Megan's work have often asked us why we are not more concerned about her spelling. If we look only at the product, it is evident that there is much that Megan cannot spell at this point.

① I am a sosara ✴ iv toked to the stars.
!! iv sreed and sotcheddnd tosts wihes iv ✴
Fund ✴ ✴ fundonnduyup Lots of Bons.
and ban to shcool. my techer was cald
Mr Buket. I Lont a grot deel from him
befror he thro ✷ me out. wun day i asked
di'g nexed this is the duk
Is the neked thay Cryed
the sosord soo the RAN and he rOnfast.
the Duk wos most.ds ta ndeed
Bi y this now is And said
I'm Going to Biy p i sid wine
weyreadyuncon hotn
that is wer It Begins

① 27.6.83

I am a sosara I've talked to the stars!

I've shuthced + shuthc and thos swiftneses iv smelt. and ive dugup lots of Bons.

Ive bean to School my teacher was Cald mr Buket.

I Lont a Great dall from Him...

Before He thro me out.

Woounday I ask the stars who was diiing nexst this is the Duk thay replied the Duk is nexsted thay Cryed so the sosara ran and He ran fast the Duk was mos

Megan—four years on and still writing.

If we consider the process, we see that she has made changes which either produce the standard forms or, in most cases, come nearer. Here is a selection.

1st draft	2nd draft	1st draft	2nd draft
sosara	sosara	bean	bean
iv	I've	shcool	school
toked	talked	cold	cald
srced/sotched	shuthced/shuthc	lont	lont
tost	thos	grat	great
swines	swiftneses	deel	dall
bons	bons	befror	before

If we were to complete this analysis we would find that in the first few pages of her story some fourteen words become standardised from one draft to the next. This is not the behaviour of a writer with a spelling problem—which is not to say that there are not words that Megan needs help to spell. The thing about the Megans of this world is that for some time to come they are going to look like poor spellers when we look at their products because they are tremendous risk takers. What they wish to write often goes beyond their spelling ability, and we tend to look at what they cannot spell rather than at what they can. The non-risk taker generally looks the better by comparison.

Assessing spelling

Since we have raised the issue of spelling, let us look a little more closely at assessment. Just as there are questions that we can ask about the writing process, so too there are questions that we can ask specifically about spelling.

Is the writer able to produce spellings that serve the purpose of recording meaning? To do this the spellings have to be sufficiently systematic for meaning to be retrieved over time. Does the writer have sufficient spelling strategies to allow this?

Does spelling interfere with the process of writing? Does a concern for spelling restrict a writer's composing?

Does the writer understand the demands of proofreading, as opposed to reading? Is the writer able to recognise non-standard forms?

Having recognised non-standard spelling, is the writer able to standardise it? If this involves recourse to a dictionary, does the writer have the alphabetic knowledge required to use one? Is the writer able to produce likely alternative spellings for a word?

Assessment that cannot be translated into classroom practice is of little real value to the classroom teacher. By highlighting specific teaching strategies for spelling and others that we believe are instrumental in the development of standard spelling, we have tried to show how we have used this kind of assessment in the classroom. We find such assessment far more helpful than that which assigns a mark out of ten. There are, unfortunately, schools where a mark is still demanded. We get round this by suggesting that spelling 'tests' be given in the form of passages to proofread which contain a certain number of non-standard words. Points can be awarded for words identified as non-standard and further points for standardisation. This is far from ideal because it still treats spelling as something apart from writing, but it does come closer to reflecting the writer's real task with spelling.

One question we are often asked is related to this issue of spelling assessment: viz. when does 'invented' spelling become a spelling problem? The question assumes that invented spelling is a stage that learners go through, but all writers invent when they do not know. There is simply more that children do not know, and because they are less experienced with language, their attempts are more likely to be non-standard. The other point about such a question is that it is product-oriented. You have a spelling 'problem' whenever the answer to the questions set out above is no. Obviously while very young writers are struggling to meet the first demand we are not going to be concerned with the others, unless their struggle also involves unwillingness to take risks. The older the writer, the greater the problem is perceived to be; nevertheless it is still the same problem.

There are two further points which relate less directly to the question of assessment. The first is that in our experience spelling problems are seldom isolated. The majority of poor spellers have reading and writing problems. Given this, it is not surprising that they have spelling problems, for spelling is but a sub-set of the broader reading and writing problems, and you cannot hope to improve spelling significantly until you tackle those broader problems. However, this is not to deny that there will be those with no reading or general writing problems who still have spelling difficulties. The second point is that while doing our best to assist these writers, we also have to develop slightly more realistic attitudes to spelling achievement. Helping them to cope with their limitations may well be a more fruitful approach.

Reporting

If we are going to adopt a process approach to assessment, it is important that we reflect this approach in our reporting to parents and other teachers. We have suggested that if we reject behaviouristic notions of learning, it is inappropriate to use a behaviouristic approach to programming. Similarly our reporting should reflect our beliefs, and talking with parent groups has shown that it can be a factor in parent education. They have been through very product-oriented language programs. Comment about process helps them to become more aware of language processes, even if it does not prevent them from focusing on the product.

Reporting of this kind demands that we keep records, since testing is not an appropriate basis for language assessment. Much has been written about the kind of records that may be kept: see, for instance, PEN 40 (Walshe 1983); *Reading Around*, 1985, no. 2. Our children did not keep records because it did not seem to be necessary, but they were constantly being asked to evaluate or comment on their own performance in one way or another. We do not deny that child-kept records may be useful to help children evaluate themselves, but we were more concerned with records that justified what we were doing to anyone outside the classroom who required such justification.

In the first instance we kept samples of children's work so that we had a selection of writing over time to discuss. We also kept process notes, which were largely anecdotal. Subsequently, however, we tried to formalise these for efficiency, and the example opposite gives some idea of how we did this. There is scope for improvement, we are sure, but our records reflected our needs at the time. Had we had the need to continue using them, they would no doubt have evolved further. It is up to teachers themselves to decide what kind of record keeping suits their needs.

Obviously records cannot be kept on every piece of writing. We reviewed each child's progress monthly. We spread our reviewing over the month so that it did not all have to be done at once. If at any time children made progress worth noting, we recorded it at that time. There is no special reason why we operated in this way: we simply found that it suited us best and gave us the information we needed, particularly in talking with parents.

NAME..... Brett. W. .... CLASS.. Family Blue (2). ....

WRITING.

1.FOCUS.

   (i) Select topic.   Yes.

   (ii) Collect information. Yes.

   (iii)Organise for writing. Difficulty organising info. needs help
                         bundling *

2.COMPOSE.

   (i) Spelling strategies.   Yes. but heavy reliance on sounding
                            out.

   (ii) Sentences & Paragraphs. Sentences ok. Paras. no existent *

   (iii)Text structure.

      Comment

      Recount

      Story   Good beginning but unable to sustain

      Report   Intrusion of personal feelings.

      Letter   Knows letter form. Good letter to Queen

   (iv) Audience & Purpose.   T.V retelling not always appropriate to task

3.EDIT.

   (i) Willingness   Yes.

   (ii) Conferences   Could use Author's Circle more. (Encourage)

   (iii)Language choice   Too much slam bam! —T.V influence.

4.PROOF-READ.

   (i) Grammar   Std.

   (ii) Spelling.
      Uses standard   Much improved
      Recognises non-standard Recognising about 60% of non-std. forms
      Corrects.   Yes with help.

   (iii)Punctuation.   Full stops o.k. Needs help with direct
                    speech.

                                    BB.

Chapter Nine

CONCLUSION

There are many contentious issues in education but few are as persistent and emotive as spelling. It is not uncommon to hear people assert that children today are not taught to spell. It is hard to unravel the assumptions and experiences that lie behind such claims because they are so confused. Certainly it has been our observation that spelling lists are still widely used. In many instances the nature of the lists used has changed to reflect children's own needs, but while this can only be applauded as a change for the better, the approach to spelling remains at heart traditional. If what people mean when they make such claims is that traditional methods are often not effective, then we would have to agree with them. It is more likely, however, that the claims merely reflect the fact that there are many who do not measure up to the degree of accuracy required by society. This has always been the case. Changing educational and employment patterns simply make poor spellers more visible.

On the other hand, it is also true that there are schools where traditional spelling practices have been abandoned and where teachers are moving towards a more language-based approach. Adults readily equate this movement with not teaching spelling at all, since most of them have only experienced a list approach. In the past we have demonstrated the importance of spelling by treating it as a separate subject and by encouraging children to write only when they had access to rudimentary standard spelling. Most adults have learned the lessons of their own schooling only too well: re-education is necessary.

Teachers cannot afford to ignore criticism, and we hoped that by working through the problem of how to teach spelling for ourselves we would be able to meet some of the criticism outlined above. We have been accused of being radical, but we believe that radicalism depends on your reference point. We do not consider starting from sound language principles radical, and this has been our starting point. We have argued that spelling is language, and that whatever is true of language in general must be true of spelling. We have examined the role of spelling within the processes of reading and writing and looked at how principles of language learning also apply in learning to spell. Such theoretical considerations, together with our observations of learners, have led us to formulate classroom practices which may appear very different from those that generally apply to the teaching of spelling at present.

Nevertheless many of the strategies we have suggested make use of time-honoured practices: there is nothing new about word study, for example. What we have sought to do is to use such practices in ways that reflect our beliefs about language and spelling—to revamp them, if you like. There are, however, some practices which have no place within our theoretical framework and we have no choice but to reject them; hence our stand on memorising lists.

Many will see this book as a book about writing and reading, and so it is. Our approach does demand one fairly radical change in thinking about spelling. For so long we have thought of spelling as an entity separate from language that it is difficult to think of it in any other way—even though we may argue that it is part of writing and reading. However, we have now arrived at a point in our understanding of written language where we can begin to work through the classroom consequences of saying that spelling is part of the writing and reading processes. Spelling must be viewed in terms of writing and reading as we have attempted to do. To talk of spelling is to talk of writing and reading. This does represent a fundamental change in attitude.

Effective change is brought about slowly. It is not only important to educate teachers; it is equally important to inform parents and gain their support. We need to be aware of parental concerns and seek to explain what we are doing, as we have emphasised a number of times. For many years parents have helped their children with spelling by 'testing' the weekly list. It was something positive they could do to assist their children's education. If we take these lists away, we must offer alternatives for them—like encouraging children to write, to have a go at possible spellings and to select standard forms.

The role of parents in implementing the program described in this book was vital. Before we began the program we talked to parents. The approach we adopted was to argue from language and language learning principles that there was a sounder way to teach spelling than the methods then used. In fact, we took parents through the table on page 7, using lots of examples from children, and through principles of language learning (Butler & Turbill 1984), making the connections between oral language, writing and spelling. We have adopted this approach with many parent groups and we find it very successful. Parents were also encouraged to assist with language activities in the classroom where possible. We had a small roster of Mums who typed stories, assisted with reading/writing activities and, above all, observed what was going on in the classroom. These parents were convinced and of course talked to other parents.

As we worked through the problem of spelling we found, not surprisingly, that we were making changes in our approach to all aspects of language. These in turn demanded changes in such areas of classroom management as:

- the physical organisation of the classroom to allow children to work co-operatively
- timetabling to allow for a block of language time so that integration could be achieved
- programming to reflect what was truly happening in the classroom rather than contriving behaviouristic objectives
- recording and reporting so that we could describe progress and account to school administration and parents for what was happening in our classroom.

With the exception of programming, these changes have been well discussed by other writers, especially Turbill (1982) and Butler & Turbill. The strategy lesson plans included in this book are examples of a possible alternative for documenting what goes on in a classroom. They not only describe strategies used but provide the rationale for using them. When linked with an overview of their use, they give a clear insight not only into what takes place in the classroom but also into a teacher's reasons for operating in this way.

We were fortunate in having a school executive which was very supportive and respected our professional judgement. Some teachers feel they are under greater constraints. That may or may not be true. The fact remains, however, that if you want the freedom to change and develop as a teacher, you have to show that you are confident in your professional judgements. It is no good arguing, for example, that a particular spelling scheme should be abandoned unless you are able to put forward a clearly articulated rationale for doing so and can suggest a different way to treat spelling. The confidence to back your professional judgement comes with experience, but this must be enhanced by reading, discussion and close observation of children. Undeniably all of this takes time and commitment, but children make it worthwhile. After one very full day of language, maths and other activities, one little boy went home and announced to his mother, 'I like being in Miss Bean's class! We do no work.' Learning is not always painless, but when children start to enjoy it, you know you are making some impact.

References

Beers, J. & Henderson, E. (1977), 'A study of developing orthographic concepts among first readers', *Research in the Teaching of English*, **11**, 2.

Butler, A. & Turbill, J. (1984), *Towards a Reading-Writing Classroom*, Primary English Teaching Association, Rozelle.

Bouffler, C. (1983), *Spelling*, Literacy Centre, Riverina-Murray Institute of Higher Education, Wagga Wagga.

Cambourne, B. (1984), 'Language, learning and literacy', *in* Butler, A. & Turbill, J., *Towards a Reading-Writing Classroom*, Primary English Teaching Association, Rozelle.

Christie, F. (1986), 'Learning to mean in writing', *in* Stewart-Dore, N. (ed.), *Writing and Reading to Learn*, Primary English Teaching Association, Rozelle.

Flower, L.S. & Hayes, J.R. (1980), 'The dynamics of composing: making plans and juggling constraints,' *in* Gregg, L.W. & Steinberg, E.R. (eds), *Cognitive Processes in Writing*, Lawrence Erlbaum Associates, Hillsdale, N.J.

Gentry, J.R. (1981), 'Learning to spell developmentally', *The Reading Teacher*, **34**, 4.

Gollasch, F. (1980), 'Readers' perception in detecting and processing embedded errors in meaningful text', unpublished doctoral thesis, University of Arizona.

____ (1986), *Micro-computers in the Whole Language Classroom*, Literacy Centre, Riverina-Murray Institute of Higher Education, Wagga Wagga.

Halliday, M.A.K. (1975), *Learning how to Mean: Explorations in the Development of Language*, Edward Arnold, London.

Harste, J.C., Woodward, V.A. & Burke, C.L. (1984), *Language Stories and Literacy Lessons*, Heinemann Educational Books, Portsmouth, N.H.

Johnson, T. & Louis, D. (1985), *Literacy through Literature*, Methuen, North Ryde.

Kohlers, P. (1968), 'Reading is only incidentally visual', *in* Goodman, K.S. & Fleming, T. (eds), *Psycholinguistics and the Teaching of Reading*, International Reading Association, Newark, Del.

Martin, J.R. & Rothery, J. (1984), *in* Rothery, J., 'The development of genres: primary to junior secondary school', Study Guide Course in *Children Writing*, Section 3, Deakin University Press, Geelong.

Murray, D.M. (1982), *Learning by Teaching: Selected Articles on Writing and Teaching*, Boynton Cook, New Jersey.

Read, C. (1975), *Children's Categorisation of Speech Sounds in English*, National Council of Teachers of English, Urbana.

Roberts, V. (1985), *Conferencing with Confidence*, PEN 53, Pri
  Teaching Association, Rozelle.
Shanklin, N.L. (1982), *Relating Reading and Writing: Developing a 1
  Theory of the Writing Process*, Monographs in Teaching and Lea
  School of Education, Indiana University, Bloomington.
Smith, F. (1982), *Writing and the Writer*, Holt, Rinehart & Winston, New York.
Turbill, J. (ed.) (1982), *No Better Way to Teach Writing!*, Primary English Teaching
  Association, Rozelle.
Walshe, R.D. (ed.) (1981), *Donald Graves in Australia: 'Children Want to Write . . .'*,
  Primary English Teaching Association, Rozelle.
____ (1983), *Evaluation of Writing*, PEN 40, Primary English Teaching Association,
  Rozelle.
Whipple, B. (1975), *Grouptalk*, Porthole Press, Belmont, Mass.
Zutell, J. (1979), 'Spelling strategies of primary school children and their relationship
  to Piaget's concept of decentration', *Research in the Teaching of English*, **13**, 1.